Anne Phillips

FOR THE LOV MIKE

Following the passing of my daughter in 2015 my perception of the final phase of grief has changed.

The dictionary defines acceptance as an acknowledgement of fact, a resignation to and reconciliation of… a bare bones definition that I have no choice but to go along with. As time has passed I have reached the sad conclusion that the fact of the deaths of my two children is indisputable. This truth my brain has grasped; my precious babes have left this earthly plane, and I must find a way to live with my reality. However…

… This definition, brutally academic and logical, does not speak to or reflect my deepest feelings. In my heart I know that I will never get over the loss of my precious children or ultimately be resigned to their untimely passing.

Having said all this, and comparing my two journeys of grief - the first twenty-four years ago and the most recent less than two years past - I can assure you, and reassure myself, that over time the hurt does lessen. I feel the raw edges of my heartbreak slowly mutate into smaller lesions that feel less painful and I begin, once again, to find the peace and joy that will carry me through the rest of my life.

Anne Hilary

Anne Hilary
April 2017

© Anne Phillips 2017
www.aheadofthegrief.me.uk

CONTENTS

Prologue — 4
My son, my Buddy — 6
A Deadly 'Game' — 8
Mike's Last Four Days — 15
What Next? — 30

Recovery from Grief Week-by-Week

Week 1 **Introduction** — 34
Week 2 **Stages of Grief** — 35
Week 3 **Shock and Denial** — 36
Week 4 **Role of Support Person** — 37
Week 5 **Early Response to Friends in Grief** — 38
Week 6 **Reliving Precious Memories** — 39
Week 7 **Crying as a Response to Grief** — 40
Week 8 **The Second Stage of Grief** — 41
Week 9 **Bereavement Groups** — 42
Week 10 **Help Through Reading and Writing** — 43
Week 11 **Yearning and Preoccupation** — 44
Week 12 **Factors Affecting our Grief Response** — 45
Week 13 **Uniqueness of Relationship** — 46
Week 14 **Recognizing Secondary Losses** — 47
Week 15 **Putting on our Comfort Coats** — 48
Week 16 **Planning for Christmas** — 49
Week 17 **Invitations and Social Gatherings** — 50
Week 18 **Coping and Healing through Symbolism** — 51
Week 19 **Multiple and Prior Loss** — 52
Week 20 **Age and Life Fulfilment Factors** — 53
Week 21 **Physiological Concerns** — 54
Week 22 **Staying Healthy and Venting Anger** — 55
Week 23 **Reactive Depression** — 56

Week 24	**The Burden of Guilt**	57
Week 25	**What about Guilt?**	58
Week 26	**Reaction vs. Response**	59
Week 27	**Grief Attacks**	60
Week 28	**Acceptance**	61
Week 29	**Spirituality and Religion**	62
Week 30	**Philosophy of Life**	63
Week 31	**Parting with Possessions**	64
Week 32	**Children in Mourning**	65
Week 33	**When Baby Loses Mum**	66
Week 34	**A Three to Five-year Old's Grief**	67
Week 35	**Answering a Child's Questions**	68
Week 36	**Emotional Benefits of the Funeral**	69
Week 37	**Reactions of Older Children**	70
Week 38	**Helping Children Work Through Grief**	71
Week 39	**The Death of a Child**	72
Week 40	**The Age of the Child... What Matter?**	73
Week 41	**Parenting the Remaining Children**	74
Week 42	**The Parents' Relationship**	75
Week 43	**Gender Differences in Grief Work**	76
Week 44	**On New Paths...**	77
Week 45	**...And on Down the Other Side**	78
Week 46	**A Fond Farewell**	79

Prologue

In 1984, after sixteen years of marriage, I took the plunge and became a single mother with custody of the youngest three of my five children: Angi and Amanda, almost three and six respectively along with Mike, nine. Cathie, 16, and Jeff, 15, stayed with their father until the following year when Cathie accepted an offer to live with the family of one of her school friends. Shortly thereafter Jeff moved in with me and his three younger siblings, making a total of five in my two-bedroom apartment. Admittedly personal space was at a premium, and I've since joked that those who retired earliest in the evening bagged the best beds!

In 1986 we moved to a nearby townhouse with three bedrooms upstairs and another that we created in the basement, which became Jeff's hangout. We had our own porch and front door, and a sliding back door leading to a small garden patch. Some would say that our living quarters were a far cry from my matrimonial home - a huge house complete with indoor pool - but the peace and freedom I found in our new home was intoxicating, and soon we all happily settled in.

During the next year I doggedly worked my way through the ramifications

of divorce, with issues of child support and weekend visitation high on the agenda. But once the legal wheels were in motion I had the time and energy to plan for the future. I needed to equip myself with the means by which I could eventually support myself and my children, and in the summer of 1987 I attended my first lecture - Course 101: An Introduction to Social Work - for which I earned my first of many top marks. I was on my way!

With two small children to care for I decided to spread my course work over four years rather than the traditional three, and my efforts to balance family life with studying paid off. I graduated with a Bachelor of Arts Degree, cum laude, then spent the next two years completing a Master's Degree in Clinical Social Work.

The topic of one of my last classes was grief and bereavement and, as instructed, I wrote the name of each of my children on five separate pieces of paper. Next we were asked to randomly select one of the slips and imagine that the name written on it was that of a loved one who had passed on. I remember being rather taken aback by the emotional reaction of several of my classmates, whereas I remained psychologically intact. Quite simply, I dismissed the whole idea as a game that was in no way, shape or form to be taken seriously. I couldn't even begin to entertain the possibility that one of my precious children would die before me! In fact, to this day I can't remember whose name I drew, so insignificant seemed the exercise.

I did find it strange, however, that only two hours of class time in six years were devoted to issues of loss through death, and now I realise how blissfully unaware I was. Within four months, when Mike had his accident, that unfathomable classroom scenario became my reality and I was unceremoniously and cruelly dropped into the bewildering abyss of grief. Worse still, neither could I ever imagine that, twenty-two years later, my youngest babe would be consumed by cancer. Once again another grief journey has been thrust upon me.

After a while and when the worst of the pain has passed, I will tell Angi's tale to remember and honour her. But for now I share snippets of Mike's life, drawn from other pieces I've written over the years. As such, I apologise in advance for any repetitive content.

I am glad of the opportunity to share the facts and pitfalls of the grief process as I learned them.

I dedicate this book to my two angels, Michael Paul and Angela Dawn. I thank them for coming to life through me and staying on earth as long as they did.

My son, my Buddy

Michael Paul Orchard was born at K-W Hospital in Kitchener, Ontario late in the afternoon of January 22, 1975. He was overdue by ten days and weighed a whopping 8lbs 13oz. The middle child of five, he was adored by his older siblings, Catharine and Jeff — just as he, in turn, lovingly welcomed his younger sisters, Amanda and Angela, into our family circle.

Mike was eager to start school and, as one of the oldest in the class, he excelled. Arithmetic was his strongest subject and at an early age he demonstrated a surprising ability to do sums in his head. He was athletic and highly competitive, and won prizes in bowling, and track and field. He skied cross-country and played t-ball and tennis. As a Beaver and then a Cub he worked hard and earned many badges.

So, too, he excelled in salesmanship, doggedly calling on repeat customers to raise funds for his school and bowling league. Few could resist those compelling deep brown eyes as he canvassed the neighbourhood with chocolate bars and other sweet treats.

Once we became a single-parent family and his older siblings had left home, Mike became my special little buddy. He helped care for his little sisters and kept them busy and safe while I studied. On Mother's Day he delighted in preparing for me a special meal, the name and ingredients of which were kept secret until served. Afterwards he basked in my praise.

At 14 he informally changed his name to Mike Phillips. He offered no explanation; neither did I ask for one. I simply took his decision as an affirmation of the close relationship we shared.

Mike had a great sense of humour and often caught me out on April Fool's day. He loved

to laugh - sometimes so hard that he made no sound at all. Then, when at last he managed to catch his breath, he laughed loudly and heartily.

He was an extremely handsome young man and, according to his orthodontist, had perfectly symmetrical features. He wore braces for two years, and only under threat of having to tolerate them even longer did he follow doctor's orders to attach the necessary elastics between top and bottom jaw. Finally his teeth were in the correct position, and off came the braces.

Even as a toddler Mike had a mind of his own. He refused to wear a bib at feeding time and, in like fashion, mastered the art of unbuckling the straps on his car seat. He once sat on the stairs for an entire morning rather than go to school in the sweater I'd chosen for him. It was one of our many battles of wits; on this occasion I lost, and Mike happily went off to school wearing a top of his own choosing.

He was a popular chap with a large circle of friends, among whom he was a leader. His nature was kind, generous and loving. He is sorely missed by all who had the privilege to know and love him.

Life cannot possibly ever be the same without you.
Thank you, my son, for the memories.

A Deadly 'Game'

Hyperventilation - the teenage killer

The church was crowded to overflowing. My mind was a blur, but I do recall standing in the church hall following Mike's memorial service, a cup of tea in one hand and an untouched sandwich in the other, staring at a sea of faces of friends and acquaintances who came to offer condolence and support. As well I remember looking into the eyes of a woman I recognised as the wife of one of Mike's teachers.

"You lost one of your sons too, didn't you? When?" I asked numbly.

"Six years ago and yesterday," she replied, and with a sniff and a sob she extended an invitation to call before giving me a hug and quickly turning away.

Sometimes it feels as if my family's hell night belongs in another lifetime; at others it seems only yesterday that my son attended a pre-Halloween party from which he never returned. In truth, it was twenty-three years ago that the coroner concluded that Mike's had been "an unfortunate, freak accident".

Blissfully unaware

It was Hell Night, the eve of that pagan festival, when Mike and six friends decided to smoke a joint. Since the hostess didn't allow such behaviour at her house, the seven found the privacy they needed on the lawn of a nearby church. After the joint was consumed one among them suggested they play a game of pass-out before rejoining the party. They began by crouching in a circle and hyperventilating. Mike was the only one who played the game well that night - so well, in fact, that when he stood up and exhaled hard, he passed out and fell backwards, hitting his head hard on the pavement.

"The blow, audible to several of his friends, knocked him out," read one newspaper report.

After a minute or so Mike regained consciousness, sat up and vomited. He rubbed the back of his head, complained of a headache and asked what had happened. One boy dashed off and returned with a car. Recognising the obvious signs of concussion, Mike's friends ignored his request to be driven home to get some sleep and headed instead for the hospital where they admitted Mike with a brief explanation about slipping on the snow or some wet leaves. Having assured Mike that he would feel better after a good night's sleep under the watchful eyes of hospital staff and arranged to see him at home the following morning, they returned to the party, blissfully unaware that their parting promise would never be kept.

The nightmare begins

Had I been at home that evening I could have been with my son during the long night while hospital staff frequently tested his reflexes and monitored his brain patterns. However, since I was staying overnight at a friend's to attend my graduation ceremony later that day, it was not until early morning that the police finally contacted me with news of the accident. When I arrived at the hospital Mike looked decidedly relieved to see me and seemed relaxed. The fact that he drifted in and out of sleep while we chatted caused me no undue concern; I simply concluded that he was tired. I began to realise the seriousness of Mike's condition only when the doctor pointed out the dark blotches on the brain scan. He seemed perplexed over the extent of the injuries, given the boys' explanation of the fall. As I signed the permission form for an immediate transfer to University Hospital an hour's drive down the highway, the gravity of the whole situation began to hit home.

There was a short delay in the transfer, allowing me, Mike's sisters and elder brother to reach the hospital before the ambulance. As the attendants raced down the hall to surgery, I ran alongside the stretcher, but my words of encouragement and love fell on deaf ears. Mike was already unconscious.

After the operation the surgeons were guardedly optimistic about Mike's prognosis, but within hours his blood pressure soared. For a second time that day he was rushed to surgery, and this time the doctors decided against replacing the piece of skull they had sawn through earlier in an attempt to relieve the pressure on Mike's bruised brain. Sadly the procedure fell short of their expectations, and while his brain continued to bleed and swell, Mike slipped deeper into his coma. Only then did his friends admit to the truth of the matter and the reason for the fall.

The vigil

For three long days we kept our vigil. I prayed for a miracle, but on the morning of the fourth day I had no choice but to give permission for all life supports to be disconnected. Again I prayed, hoping against the odds that Mike's lungs would resume their life-giving task. Again my prayers went unanswered. Within minutes his chest heaved and fell one last time. I had a sense of Mike's spirit wafting past me towards one corner at the ceiling. The tiny room became deathly quiet and my son's body lay deathly still.

Mike was gone, and all I had left were memories of that handsome eighteen-year-old who loved life and lived it to the full. He was a selfless, willing child to whom I turned for help in our single-parent home. He patiently taught me how to use my first computer and fixed minor problems on my car. We moved often since the divorce and Mike's job, among others, was to hook up the stereo and television equipment. He worked the Saturday night shift at McDonald's to relieve our family's financial pressures; at the same time he aimed for a school average high enough to secure a place in the mechanical engineering program at the university his two older siblings and I had attended. Mike would have made a good engineer, given his curiosity of the way things worked, his innate mathematical ability and penchant for giving any challenge his all. And therein lies the irony; so well did he play that final game that it cost him his life.

During the succession of long dark days and nights that followed, I bounced between the inevitable stages of grief, invariably revisiting the first phase of shock and disbelief. In my numbness I played a game with myself, rewinding and replaying the mental tapes that my confused mind created once the facts and events of that fateful night were revealed. In my desire to end the nightmare by constructing a different ending, I attached an *if only* to the beginning of each tape. *If only* they hadn't gone out to smoke that joint. *If only* he'd been facing the other way and landed on the soft grass. *If only* he hadn't been so tall and the patch of grass so small. *If only* the girls had told me they'd watched Mike and his friends play the game at home. *If only* someone had warned me of the dangers of hyperventilation games. And at the very least, *if only* I'd known he would slip away so soon and been with him in the ambulance during his last moments of consciousness.

The facts

At the inquest six months later I began to understand the facts around hyperventilation games, more commonly called 'pass-out' or 'black-out' by the generation that plays them. As one after another of Mike's companions took the stand, we heard evidence to the fact that such activities are not an uncommon occurrence, especially among adolescent boys. I learned, also, that there are several ways, other than the method Mike had used, to experience the high that causes the passing out.

"You bend over and take a deep breath, then stand up and have a friend push hard on your chest. Then you faint and fall down," one girl told the court after admitting to playing the game on occasion and watching it on several others. "They call it the funky chicken," she added, referring to the convulsive-like movements that result. She went on to explain that even though it takes only a few seconds to come around, it feels as if two hours have passed.

The witnesses' remarks supported those I had read in an article included in the newspaper coverage of Mike's accident, compiled from a statement by a local parent who reported observing groups of youths playing the game.

"They'd hold a child against a wall and put their hands against his neck. His whole body would go limp and shake about. Then he would get up really slowly," the woman had stated, corroborating Mike's friends' description of the convulsions.

Once each witness was questioned to the court's satisfaction, a specialist in lung disorders took the stand to apprise the jurors of the medical facts. He explained the process by which a grand mal seizure occurs and, as in Mike's case, an unprotected fall: forced inhalation and exhalation lower carbon dioxide levels in the blood, in turn decreasing blood flow to the brain through

the narrowed vessels. As such, the expert concluded, the game is a dangerous one and can, at the very least, cause brain damage each time it is played.

The jurors' unanimous findings took the form of two recommendations on the basis of the apparent increasing incidence of injuries and/or death following hyperventilation.

The first, directed towards the Ministry of Health, was that information be disseminated to the public by distribution of pamphlets, literature, displays and other media. Secondly, school boards should be made aware of the medical facts and repercussions of the dangers of hyperventilation games performed by adolescents who fail to realise the seriousness of this practice. To this end, the jurors also suggested that some of those who had experienced such situations might conduct formal presentations in class.

Time for change

Having relived the events of that fateful night, minute-by-minute, I left the courthouse feeling emotionally drained but with the satisfaction that Mike's death might have some meaning if young lives could be saved and other families spared the heartache of such senseless and devastating loss. In that respect the three-day ordeal had given me a sense of closure and a pivotal point from which to get on with my life.

Being all too familiar with the frightening reality of the fragility of life, my daughters and I moved to a farmhouse where I found the space and peace I needed to begin work on my first book. Simultaneously I wrote a weekly bereavement column for the local newspaper - a project that helped me, as much as it did my readers, to navigate the seemingly unending grief process.

During those painful two years more tragic accounts of death through hyperventilation came to my notice, prompting me to investigate further. Two meetings - one with the deputy coroner and another with a school head - confirmed my suspicions that inquest recommendations are only as good as their follow-up. In Mike's case, the file had been tied up with red tape, passed between the relevant authorities and eventually buried on bureaucracy's back shelf. Along with the revelation that the inquest had seemed to be a waste of time came the realisation that I needed to write Mike's story.

An awareness campaign

I continue to seek closure by sharing the facts as I painfully learned them. The playing of hyperventilation games is not unlike alcohol and drug abuse in that it is a secret well kept until tragedy strikes. As parents and educators we must strive to be informed if we are to protect our children to the best of our ability. While there are no guarantees that we can keep our children safe outside of the home, we must assume responsibility by warning them of certain dangers, possibly by relating other families' stories. Most importantly, we need to keep the lines of communication open within our families and be vigilant of telltale signs of otherwise secretive activities.

One last fact I would like to share is that the potentially deadly game is not a thing of the past, proof of which I gathered through an interview with a local youth who admitted to playing the game on school property. The after effects of oxygen deprivation to his brain - mini-blackouts and temporary loss of vision - had made him think twice before playing the game again. Perhaps this young man is alive and well today because he knew enough to delegate his friends as catchers before he passed out and fell. Mike was neither so knowledgeable nor lucky.

I had already sent Mike's story to countless parent and child magazines in Canada, the USA and UK. All submissions were politely turned down, often with sincere condolences and the same reasons: the story did not fit the magazine's vision, and all issues for the foreseeable future were already in the pipeline. However, when I resubmitted Mike's story, exclusively to the UK market, along with the witness statement, it was published in 'Headlines', the Journal of the Secondary Heads Association, UK, November 2002.

"We speak for the dead to protect the living," reads the framed motto hanging in the coroner's office. I'm betting that if Mike could speak for himself, his words would echo mine…

"If only I'd known…".

Mike's Last Four Days

My unspoken thoughts in italics

Sunday, October 31 1993, 5am

Ring... ring... ring... ring... ring... ring... ring... ring... ring... ring...

What's that? Not my alarm! Oh no, it's the phone. Who's calling at this early hour? It's not even light out. Uh oh, it must be bad news. I don't think it's for me. I sure hope not.

I hear Ben answer in the next room and then open my door. "Anne, it's for you..."

For me? Who is it? What's happened now?

My heart beats faster as I jump out of bed. The girls, in the bed beside me, are already awake.

"Hello?"

"Mrs. Phillips-Orchard?"

"Yes?"

"This is officer... Waterloo police... your son Mike..."

Oh no, it's Mike! I knew it. It's always about Mike. Oh dear, now what?

"He's been in the emergency ward in Kitchener since ten o'clock last night. He slipped shovelling snow and hit his head..."

"Snow? I didn't know it snowed!"

"Actually very little... a sprinkling... but that's what his friends reported when they took him to the hospital. He's being monitored, and we've been trying to locate you all night... at your Hamilton residence."

Just monitoring! I guess they're keeping him in as a precaution. Phew! It doesn't sound so bad. Thank goodness for that!

I say I'll head for the hospital. I hang up and peek outside. There's a sprinkling of snow on the leaves but hardly enough to need clearing. From the light in the hallway I pull on yesterday's clothes. The girls are sitting up.

They look worried and questioning, but after hearing what the officer had to say, I'm feeling a little less stressed.

"It's Mike. He's slipped and bumped his head. I'll call as soon as I've seen him."

Even though I've told the girls not to worry, as always happens when I hear of a child of mine in distress, I'm worried. My heart is pounding as I drive to the hospital and park in the empty gas station across the road. My hands are shaking as I rest them on the check-in counter. The nurse acts mildly disinterested when I tell her who I am and ask to see Mike. She tells me to take a seat.

> "It's Mike. He's slipped and bumped his head..."

Now what does that mean? Does she know something but doesn't want to be the one to tell me? No, she's probably just doing her job and doesn't know anything about Mike.

After a few minutes she says I can go in. I tell a nurse I'm Mike Phillips' mum and am led towards a bed on the far side of the room. Mike's lying still with his eyes closed but opens them when I speak. He looks pale and a little spaced out, I assume because he's been sleeping. My heart rate slows down a little.

Well, he looks okay, so I guess he IS okay. Thank goodness! Another bump on the head, that's all!

He says he has a headache and I can see he's upset — just as Angi was when I arrived at this same hospital and found her having the cut on her head stitched up years ago. I hold Mike's hand, assure him he'll be okay and promise to stay with him. The nurse approaches, checks Mike's chart and asks him what day it is.

"Halloween... and mum's graduation day," he answers almost immediately, although his voice sounds weak.

"Good! Very good," she says as she writes on the sheet. "Now mum's here, he's more responsive."

Good! Oh good! He's not too bad if he can remember that, and he's already feeling better! So he IS going to be okay!

The nurse tells me they've been assessing Mike every half hour and adds that the doctor would like to speak with me. I follow her to a work station on the other side of the room and am surprised to see my mother's GP. He looks surprised to see me too, and recognises me from the many times I took my mother to his surgery.

"Yes, of course. Phillips!" he exclaims as he clips what looks like a skull x-ray onto the light panel attached to the wall. "Mike seems stable right now, but on his CAT scan... do you see these dark patches?"

I nod and feel my heart beat faster.

"Mike's head's taken a pretty hard bash, and these spots indicate bruising to the brain, and some bleeding. Here too..." he points with his pencil at more dark splotches on a second scan. I nod and wait in silence as he turns to face me.

"The neurosurgeon wanted to admit Mike to ICU earlier and monitor him there, as we've been doing all night here. But..." he hesitates and looks directly into my eyes, "... as the attending doctor, the decision was mine to keep him here in emergency until you could be contacted. The police have been trying to find you all night!"

> *"I mean... are his injuries that bad?"*

I know. I know. I wasn't at home. I was here in Waterloo only five minutes away, and my son's been here all alone all night. And the doctor looks so worried, like I should be worrying too. And I am. Oh dear, Mike's injuries must be worse than I thought.

"At London University Hospital they have better diagnostic equipment..." he goes on, and I get the impression he wants to say more. When he doesn't, I follow his cue.

"So... you think Mike would be better off in London? I mean... are his injuries that bad?"

"It's hard to know right now just how serious, but that's what I recommend," he says, bringing my attention back to the dark blotches. "It could be that he'd be fine here... but just to be on the safe side... and as Mike's mother, it's up to you."

It's up to me? Why is that? Surely he knows better! Oh, I see. This is about hospital politics and a professional difference of opinion. I have to be the one to say it.

"Yes, of course. From what you've told me, I'd like Mike moved to London."

The doctor looks relieved and goes off to order an ambulance. I return to Mike's bedside. He opens his eyes when I take his hand. I carefully choose my words to explain what's happening next.

I hope Mike doesn't get upset. I hope I can put this so that he doesn't.

"Mikey, the doctor says they could treat you here... but it might be better for you to be in hospital in London. They've got better equipment there to make sure they don't miss anything. And I'll stay with you until the ambulance comes."

He seems too groggy to respond but nods before he closes his eyes. The doctor comes over to say there will be a slight delay in getting an ambulance, and since Mike appears to be sleeping I leave to find a pay phone to call John, Mike's dad. It's still early, especially for a Sunday, but he answers quickly, and I assume his response to an early morning call is much like mine. Briefly I fill him in. He questions the reason for Mike's fall, and I tell him I think it sounds strange too. He says he'll meet us in London later on. I hang up, buy a coffee from the machine and go outside for a cigarette. Five minutes later I go back inside.

The wait is longer than I thought it would be, and I wish they'd hurry up and get Mike to where he needs to be. The nurse assures me that the ambulance won't be long coming now. She wakes Mike up, asks a few simple questions and makes tick marks on a new column. Again Mike closes his eyes, and she explains about the assessment sheet they use for patients with brain injuries. After she finishes I decide to leave. I'd rather stay with Mike, but I need to get back to Ben's and pack a few things. I want to get to London before Mike does and besides, I know the girls must be worrying.

"Okay Mike, they'll be here soon," I tell him. He opens his eyes, looks at me and then closes them again. "We'll see you in London, okay buddy?"

> *I kiss his forehead and give his hand a squeeze*

Mike opens his eyes again to acknowledge that he heard. I kiss his forehead and give his hand a squeeze. I'm beginning to feel numb as I exit through the automatic door and cross the empty road. I feel as if I'm watching myself playing the lead role in an unfolding drama. Tears form in the corner of my eyes as I drive up King Street.

No! No! Don't get upset. There's no reason to get upset. Mike's going to London, and the doctor said he'll be okay there. He did, didn't he? Yes he did, I'm sure he did. Anyway, Mike's always been okay before, so he will be this time too!

The girls are already dressed and eating breakfast with Ben. I join them although I'm not hungry. I fill them in and assure them that their brother will be just fine. I phone Jeff to tell him what's happened and arrange to pick him up. His girlfriend, Anna, is in Waterloo for my graduation and will come along too.

> *...I have the feeling we're all pushing fearful thoughts aside*

The girls drive with Ben, and Jeff and Anna ride with me. I watch for the ambulance. It doesn't pass, and I wonder if it's behind us or in front. The conversation is about this and that, and I have the feeling we're all pushing fearful thoughts aside. We park, and I check in at the admissions desk. I'm surprised Mike hasn't yet arrived but glad I'll be there when he does. I join the others in a waiting room down the hall and, after it feels like too much time has passed, I return to the desk.

"Oh, there you are!" the nurse exclaims before I have a chance to ask the question. "Mum's here!" she calls to the ambulance attendants standing just inside the doors.

Oh, there he is! He's here, and we've been waiting over there. What the hell?

A clipboard is thrust at me, and I sign the sheet without reading it. The nurse has already told me it's an authorisation for surgery.

Not surgery! He needs surgery already? Oh my God! What's going on?

The attendants are already wheeling the gurney, and Mike, in my direction. I walk quickly towards them.

Hey, wait just a minute! I want to give my son a hug and a kiss. I want him to know I'm here with him and that everything will be alright. I want to tell him I love him. Hey, slow down!

But they keep on going, and I'm hurrying to catch up. Now I'm running along beside him.

"Mike. Hi Mike..." I call out. But a nurse tells me to get out of the way.

Why is Mike's hair soaking wet? And why is he unconscious? Wait!

The procession's gone before I get a chance to talk to Mike or ask questions. I go back to the waiting room. I'm stunned and confused but manage to tell the rest what has happened. I can see they feel as I do. Then the same nurse comes back to apologise.

"I'm so sorry... we had to get your son to surgery right away," she explains, kneeling in front of me and taking my hand. "He suffered a bleed in the ambulance... and the seizure caused him to sweat a lot."

He sweated so much that his hair's soaking wet? Or maybe they threw a bucket of water over him to cool him down? What's going on?

"But he's young and fit and has the strength to come through this," she tells me, and I have no choice but to believe her. I have to believe her!

The wait is excruciating. I phone Andrew, my nephew, to tell him where I am and that I won't be attending my graduation. I ask him to phone my mother and promise to call again as soon as I have some news. As I hang up I give myself a mental pat on the back for managing to sound so calm. I'm still play-acting my way through the drama.

At long last the surgeon appears and gathers us in a quiet room. He says Mike has come through the operation and explains that they removed a piece of his skull, inserted shunts to drain off the excess blood to relieve the pressure on his brain, then put the piece of bone back in place. We all breathe a sigh of relief. I thank him, but our relief is short-lived.

"Although, as I said, your son's condition is stable... I don't want you thinking he's out of the woods," he cautions. "Any complication... a further build-up of pressure... could precipitate another emergency."

> *"... a further buildup of pressure could precipitate another emergency"*

His tone frightens me as much as his words, but my fear recedes a little when he ends the briefing on a positive note. He repeats that Mike's condition is presently stable, and the nurse's assurance that youth and strength are on his side come to mind.

Yes, that's right! She did say that, and it's true. So he's going to pull through!

Now that Mike is over the first big hurdle, we head for the cafeteria — except Ben who leaves to call on his niece. She lives in a large house only blocks from the hospital, and he intends to ask her if the girls and I can stay there until Mike's condition improves.

Jeff, Anna and I order the soup of the day. There are large pieces of mushrooms floating in a thick light-brown sauce, and I'm the only one who likes it. I'm still not hungry, but eating seems a normal thing to do in the midst of chaos. As I eat I lose track of the conversation and conjure up a comforting vision.

When Mike's better I'll take him home... not to Waterloo, but Hamilton. He can have my bedroom, and I'll bunk in the attic with the girls. We'll be one big happy family again! After what he's been through, he'll need a lot of care, and I'll nurse him back to health. Thank goodness I haven't found a job yet! Oh, I can hardly wait to get him home!

I phone my mother who's relieved to hear Mike is doing okay following surgery. I don't elaborate on the doctor's warning, perhaps as much for my own benefit as hers. I'm surprised to learn that Andrew, Jane, Jennifer (my niece) and Graham are there with her; she explains that since they were planning on attending my graduation they made the trip to Waterloo anyway. I'm glad they're there with her.

Ben returns with news that Joanne will be happy to accommodate us and says he will return to Waterloo now that Mike is stable. Jeff and Anna decide to ride back with him. I need to follow Ben to Joanne's because I don't know where she lives, but first I want to see Mike if I'm allowed to.

At the door of the intensive care unit, I have to press a button and talk through the speaker in order to gain entrance. Once inside I find Mike's bed past the nurses' station and to the right. I stand watching him, not quite knowing what to make of the situation. His head is completely bandaged, and there are many tubes and wires attached to Mike and the machines circling the head of his bed. A nurse hovers, checking the dials and intermittently adjusting the apparatus.

> *...I know that the machine is breathing for him*

Oh Mike, you poor boy. Look what's happened to you! Whatever were you doing to get so badly hurt? And look... they've shaved off all your hair, and only a few days ago you said it would soon be long enough to wear in a pony tail! But you look good... all pink and peaceful, as if you're sleeping. I know you're not, and soon you'll wake up. Please wake up soon. Please?

I hold his hand and watch his chest rise and fall. His breathing is quiet and even, but I know that the machine is breathing for him.

Mike, I don't know if you can hear me. I hope so because I want you to know I love you, and how frightened I've been. But I'm here with you now, and you're going to be okay. When you wake up and they say you can go home, I'll take you to Hamilton and look after you until you're completely better.

I don't know what else to say, and Ben's waiting to be on his way. I kiss Mike's warm cheek and smell the sweetness of his skin. I bring my mouth close to his ear, just in case he might hear me better.

"I love you, Mike, and I'll be back soon. 'Bye love."

I stroke his hand and glance back once as I pass the nurses' station.

> *Mike, I don't know if you can hear me. I hope so...*

I haven't seen Joanne in quite some time, and she's friendly and welcoming. She has a toddler who the girls can play with. After the others leave, the girls and I sit in the kitchen while she makes coffee. She asks Amanda and Angi if they're going out for Halloween. They tell her their outfits are back in Waterloo, and she offers to find something for them to wear if they want to go out. They say they do. She invites them upstairs but first puts a frozen turkey in the oven. I can't imagine it will be ready in time for dinner, but I think I still won't be hungry anyway. Once the girls and Joanne go off to search through her closet, I don't know what to do with myself.

Maybe I'll go up and watch and try to get into the spirit of the thing. No, I'm feeling too antsy to get involved in anything so trivial... I don't mean trivial to the girls, and it will be good for them to go out. I wonder how Mike's doing? Maybe he's awake by now. Wouldn't that be wonderful? Or maybe he'll wake up soon, and I want to be there when he does. Yes, I'm going back. I don't think the girls will mind.

They understand, and I promise to be back in time to see them in their costumes. As always on Halloween, the weather is dull and chilly, and I shiver as I walk the three blocks. I reach the entrance to the long hospital driveway just as a car approaches, but only once it's passed do I realise it was John and Diane. An ominous chill runs through me, and I pick up my pace.

At ICU I press the buzzer and ask to be let in. I'm told to wait. I don't understand why but presume Mike's nurses are working with him, and I would be in their way. I sit and wait five minutes before pressing the buzzer again. I don't want to be a bother, but my son's in there, and I need to be with him.

Again I'm told to wait, and my imagination catches fire.

Something's gone wrong! Really wrong! I know it! Why else won't they let me in? They don't want me to know what's happening. Oh please, please let me in and let him be okay. I can't just sit here. I don't care if they get mad at me. I'm going to buzz again.

This time I'm allowed in, but the flurry around Mike's bed keeps me on the periphery. I watch as one nurse checks his blood pressure. Another is working in behind on one of the machines. Finally, a third nurse notices me and explains that Mike's blood pressure is up and he's on his way to surgery again. I ask no questions while the wires are reconnected to smaller portable machines. I step back out of the way as they wheel Mike's bed past me and out of sight.

Mike's blood pressure is up and he's on his way to surgery again.

I can't leave, but I can't stay here alone while Mike's in surgery again. I'm crying as I phone Ben. He asks if I want him to come back, and I tell him I do. He says he's on his way. Then I phone Joanne and speak to the girls. They tell me they don't care about Halloween and say they'll walk over to the hospital. The waiting room is empty except for me, and I spend the time composing a scenario that caused Mike's blood pressure to soar.

He was stable when I left this afternoon. Did he know John and Diane were here? Did they say something that upset him? Did he try to respond and got frustrated when he couldn't? Is that why his blood pressure began to soar? In any case that would mean he can hear me... or at least he could when I saw him earlier on. I hope so but I don't know. I just don't know. But now he's even worse than he was before. Oh dear... please will something good happen? Please?

I'm still musing when the girls arrive and I'm glad they're here. I tell them their father and step-mother have visited but spare them the details of my imaginings. As we sit and wait for Mike to be brought back from surgery, a hospital chaplain comes to take us down to a family room on the main floor. He says he's concerned about us and that we can wait there rather than in the waiting room. I ask if we can sleep there.

"Usually we don't allow the room to be used for sleeping overnight in case another family needs to share it…"

I feel let down and a bit angry and tell him we're staying at the hospital all night and will sleep in the waiting room if we have to. At that he gives us permission to use the family room for one night. Ben finds us there as does an office worker delivering a fax. It's from Andrew; he must be back home by now. In the first paragraph he asks that I read the note to Mike.

I glance down the page. He's saying he's only recently been reunited with his cousin and wants to get to know him better. He talks about the strength and joy of life he saw in Mike the day we moved and implores him to hang on. Through my tears I can barely make out the words, but they bring home the bitter truth. Mike's in big trouble!

Ben has brought along our bags, as well as dinner in a Tupperware container. It's turkey and vegetables, and we take it up to the cafeteria and find some plates and cutlery. The counter is closed, and we're the only ones present. It feels cold and stark, and the girls and I aren't hungry. It's been a long day and we're all tired, but we're waiting for Mike to come back from surgery before we try to get some sleep.

We return to ICU. Mike's back and we're allowed in. I stare mindlessly at a nurse with a carpenter's level in her hand. She moves it up and down close to the right side of Mike's head. She notices I'm watching and explains she's trying to find the right level for one of the machines. Mike looks the same as before, and I've already been told that this time they didn't replace the piece of his skull, to give his swelling brain more room.

It's getting worse, and I don't think he's going to get better! I know it. I feel it. The doctor sounds even more worried now than he did this morning. Oh my God! What are we going to do? What are we going to do without Mike?

I share my fears with Ben before he leaves for Joanne's, but not in front of the girls. He says Mike has every chance of recovering. I want to believe him more than anything else in the world, and I know he's trying to help. One thing I do know is that I'm grateful he's back.

The doctor sounds even more worried now...

We bunk down on the two black leather couches. They've given us two pillows and light blankets, and I'm glad I'm sharing my couch with Angi because we're warmer together than apart. There's not much room for the two of us; she's lying on the inside, and I pull a coffee table close so I have somewhere to put my left leg. I lie on my back, wide awake, and clutch Mike's school picture that I carry in my wallet. I hold it over my heart. I recite The Lord's Prayer over and over again and add my own supplications.

Our Father, who art in heaven, hallowed be thy name... Please God, please save my son. I'll do anything you ask and never ask you for anything else. I'll quit smoking and anything else I shouldn't be doing. Only please don't let him die...

> *It's eerily quiet in the hospital hallways...*

I sleep fitfully for short periods. Each time I wake up I repeat my prayer then go to see Mike. It's eerily quiet in the hospital hallways and the elevator's always empty except for me. In ICU, the lights are dazzlingly bright and hurt my eyes. Every time I get buzzed in I'm hopeful that Mike will show some signs of life, and each time he doesn't I'm more sure he never will. I don't stay long, and yet I can't seem to stop myself from going back again and again and again.

Monday, November 1

I wish I could take a shower. I think I'd feel a bit better if I could, but I clean myself up as best I can. I stare into the mirror and hardly recognise the face gazing back at me.

Who are you? Surely you're not Anne! She should have a happy face. She was supposed to graduate yesterday. All her children, except for Cathie, were going to be there to congratulate her and tell her they're proud of her. She was going to get cards and flowers. So who's this sad woman staring back at me from the mirror in a hospital washroom?

Ben's back at the hospital, and soon Jeff arrives with my friend, Irene, and her son. I'm surprised to see them because she's had surgery which would have prevented her from attending my graduation. But she says she had to come to London, despite the pain she's in, and I appreciate that. Also I'm thankful that Joanne's house, and her heart, is big enough to put everyone up.

John is in ICU when I get there and asks if I know the actual reason that Mike fell. I tell him I heard it wasn't snow he slipped on, but leaves. He says Mike's friends have finally told the truth — that they smoked a joint and then played a game.

Snow or leaves? And a game? But what does it matter what caused the accident?

Mike fell, he's fighting for his life, and we're all here praying he wins. That's all I'm thinking about and all that matters. And I'm scared... so scared.

There's another meeting in a quiet room. Jeff sits one side of me and Irene on the other. I'm glad she's here, especially since she's a nurse and can tell me what's going on, in layman's terms. The doctors explain to John and Diane why they didn't replace the piece of Mike's skull and add that even so, his brain is still swelling and bleeding. Their tone is ominous, and I sense the rest are as frightened as I am.

> I'd rather drink coffee and smoke than eat.

I eat very little of my breakfast and feel physically sick. I'd rather drink coffee and smoke than eat. I spend the morning going between ICU, the front entrance to the hospital and the quadrangle at the back. It's a bleak wintry day but I hardly feel the cold. Mid-afternoon I am talked into returning to Joanne's and taking a nap. I lie on the couch in the living room, next to the kitchen where Ben and his sister, Mary, are chatting. They're using quiet voices, but the few words I catch send me into a panic.

Oh no. Please no! She's talking about how I'm going to need a lot of support, and Ben's agreeing. I knew it! I've known all along Mike's not going to make it, even though they all keep telling me he is. Now they think I can't hear them and are saying what they really think. But I can't go there! I don't dare go to that place in my head where I know Mike's going to die. If I do I'll go totally mad and never ever get sane again. So I must not think, I must not think, I must not think, I must not think.

I doze until the pizza delivery boy, ringing the door bell, wakes me up. I feel a little better for the nap and am glad of the food and the company. It feels surreal to be eating and chatting around Joanne's kitchen table, and I wonder if I'm not the only one who's not daring to 'go there'. I wish Mike was here too and, for a short while, pretend he is. But he's not.

Back at the hospital I see a familiar couple step off the elevator, and it takes me a few seconds to recognise Cathie's parents-in-law.

What a coincidence to see them both here. Are they visiting somebody as well? Yes, that must be it. But no, they're here because of Mike of course, and that's how serious this all is.

They ask after Mike and tell me Chris and Cathie are flying in tonight. Tomorrow we'll all be together.

It's late evening, and I go to the hospital pharmacy to ask for something to help me and the girls sleep. I can't understand why the pharmacist is asking so many questions. All I'm asking for is enough medication to get us through the next couple of nights. Eventually he hands over six pills, and we head back to Joanne's.

Tuesday, November 2nd

The girls and I slept a little better, together on Joanne's pull-out couch with me in the middle. The pills helped, as did my being able to feel and touch the girls the few times I awoke in the darkness. We head back to the hospital. I ask the nurse why Mike's hand is so cold, and she explains he's lying on a pad of ice to keep his body temperature down. Apparently the part of his brain that's supposed to do that isn't working. I tell the nurse I don't like the thought of him being so cold, and she promises to move the pack. The next time I hold his hand it feels warmer. He's covered from toes to mid-chest with a white sheet, and I can see that his tummy's bloated. Again the nurse offers an explanation and a solution: Mike's body is retaining fluid, which will soon be drained.

Cathie and Chris are here now, and they attend the morning's meeting in a quiet room. There are so many of us around the table — everyone except Amanda and Angi who are being spared the details. The doctors drone on.

> ...they need to keep Mike's corneas lubricated so they can be transplanted.

Okay. Okay. I hear you. What? Now you're asking for permission to unplug Mike's breathing machine? Oh no! Please no! But yes! And yes, Mike did sign the back of his driver's licence. Yes, he wants to donate all his body parts upon his death. Death! When? Soon! His brain is dead. Soon he'll be dead. Not today though. Tomorrow. Are you sure? They're sure. Okay, tomorrow.

My good friend, Bobbie, has arrived and is here in the quadrangle as well. It's even colder today. Back inside I note that Mike's tummy is now flat beneath the smooth white sheet. Every so often the nurse pulls down the bottom lid of his eyes to put in drops. Irene explains that they need to keep Mike's corneas lubricated so they can be transplanted.

Okay, that's it. This is not a bad dream. It's an honest-to-goodness nightmare. No more kidding yourself, Anne. The reality is that Mike IS going to die!

I put one foot in front of the other and time after time find myself standing beside my sweet son's bed. I talk to him but don't know what I'm saying. I kiss his cheek. I leave and come back again. On a payphone I call the minister at our church. He assures me that he and a colleague will visit my mother and tell her the news.

> Today is the day my son is to die.

Wednesday, November 3rd

Today is the day my son is to die. But he's only 18! And it's Amanda's 14th birthday. How could I have forgotten? I'm sorry, Amanda, even though you say it's okay that your brother will die on your birthday. It's not okay, and I'm so sorry.

There's another meeting in a quiet room. Mike has one reflex left, which means he can't be pronounced brain dead, which also means he won't be donating his main body organs, which then means that only his corneas, long bones and skin will be harvested.

Harvested! Harvested? What an odd word to use! And of all the reflexes to be the last, of course it's Mike's gagging reflex. Didn't he always have a tough time when the orthodontist put wax in his mouth to make impressions for moulds for his braces? He had them on for so long because he didn't like wearing the elastics. But I bugged him about it, and now his teeth are perfect. Wasted effort... wasted time... wasted life! And didn't he gag in the back of the car and ask to stop so he could vomit outside? I remember, and so does Irene. So many memories, and it's his sister's birthday as well.

John asks me, Jeff and Cathie to go to a quiet room with him. First I visit Mike.

I can't save you Mike, and I'm sorry. I'm your mum and supposed to keep you safe and alive. I'd give anything to be able to, but I can't. Now it's too late to expect you to wake up. It's too late to kid myself that I can take you home. And look! Look at your poor head... your poor face! It's such a strange shape without that extra piece of your skull. You're still beautiful, but we can't put you back together again. Humpty Dumpty sat on a wall, Humpty Dumpty had a great fall. I'm so sorry... and now your dad wants me to go to the quiet room with Jeff and Cathie.

We wait for John to speak, but he's having trouble getting started.

So what's he going to say? That he's sorry for all he did and said to Mike? That will be something to see and hear, I must say! What's he going on about now? That we have to look after the girls? What does he mean? Of course we have to look after them! Oh, right. He feels guilty about the way he treated Mike and wants to make up for it. I guess that makes sense, and that's all he has to say.

We all exit the little room, but soon I find myself back inside with the hospital chaplain who set us up in the family suite that first night. We talk about Jesus and God, life, death and heaven, until someone raps on the door. It's Cathie urging me to hurry.

Already? Only a few minutes left you say? Oh no! Only one more chance to talk to him... to say goodbye. Dear God... no!

The chaplain and I find Mike in a small curtained area in a different section of the ward. The others are already there, except Amanda and Angi. I stand in my usual spot and hold Mike's left hand. The intravenous needle has gone along with the breathing apparatus and the other machines, except for the heart monitor. In fact, without so many tubes and wires I could almost believe Mike's just sleeping.

But he's not sleeping. He's in a coma and he's dying. Angi and Amanda should be here! They love their brother so much, and they're old enough to be here with us while he dies. I'll go get them. No I can't. Mike's having trouble breathing so there's no time, and it would seem rude to leave in the middle of the prayers.

> *...the machine is silent and the green line is flat.*

I watch Mike's chest rise and fall. I'm still standing close beside him but feel as if I'm watching from a great distance.

That's it, Mike. Keep on breathing. In and out. Keep on trying. Come on, you can do it. Please. Up and down. In and out. Uh oh, that last breath was noisier and it took you a long time to draw it in. Oh, how can I make you keep on breathing? There must be something I can do. But there isn't. No, please don't let that shuddering breath be your last gasp? I think it is... I think it was... and now the machine is silent and the green line is flat like in Flatliner, one or your favourite movies.

I feel my son's sweet spirit cross in front of me and disappear up past the curtains to my left. I kiss his cheek and whisper 'I love you'. With my fingertips I gently touch his yellow lips. They feel rubbery as I remember my sister's did as she lay in her coffin.

'Bye Mike. I love you, my little buddy. No sense staying here any longer. It's over. It's time to get the girls and head home...

We leave, but this time I don't look back.

What next?

Our beloved son and brother was gone leaving me, Amanda and Angi bereft and lost. We had left Waterloo - the city in which the girls had lived their entire lives - and rented an apartment in Hamilton only two months before Mike's accident. Now we felt like aliens in a city we'd once hoped to call home. Daily we muddled on, each trying to cope with our sadness in unique ways and supporting one another as best we could. Angi bravely returned to school, but Amanda couldn't bring herself to do the same. In January we spent two weeks in England visiting my family - a trip that was planned before Mike died. In March we drove to Florida and spent three weeks at my mother's winter home. But each time on our return, the consensus was that we needed a complete change in location and lifestyle. Basically, Mike's death brought home the obvious fact that life is sometimes too short, and often too changeable, to make less than the best of it.

So it was that we began our search for a country home where the girls could indulge their love of animals - dogs, cats, guinea pigs, mice, rats and cats - to their hearts' content. Also, having taken riding lessons for many years, they placed horses high on their agenda.

One sunny Saturday early in June we drove twenty miles south towards Lake Erie and stopped for coffee at a diner in Hagersville. On our table there happened to be a copy of a weekly newspaper in which we found an advert for a farmhouse, well within our budget, for rent. The waitress, who happened to be familiar with the property, gave us directions and off we hurried to take a look.

A perfect country home

We easily located the house two miles south towards Jarvis and instantly fell in love with that two-storey red brick dwelling set back from the road and surrounded by fields. We parked, boldly knocked at the back door and, when nobody answered, unabashedly peeked through the windows. We liked what we saw: a big old-fashioned farm kitchen papered in dainty blue flowers with a matching border of yellow ducks; a dining room with ample space for table and desks; and a lounge large enough for our living room furniture with room to spare. At the entrance to both the kitchen and dining room were smaller add-ons - roomy nooks to hang coats and leave muddy boots.

Next we checked out the barn and, as if finding several stalls wasn't excitement enough, we came upon a paddock and two ponies grazing. As the girls, with eyes as big as saucers and wide grins, perched on the fence railings and stroked the animals' soft noses, I sensed we'd found our perfect home!

Happily, and with the thought that our dreams could possibly become reality, we paused at the end of the driveway and gazed longingly back at the house. We named it *Gingerbread House* due to its isolation, simplicity and scalloped wooden trim at the roof line.

Because I was unemployed, and a single-parent to boot, I worried that our application might be passed over in favour of seemingly more reliable tenants. But I kept my fearful thoughts to myself and promised the girls I would do all I could to make this dream home our own. As instructed in the ad I wrote a letter outlining our circumstances. I pulled out all the stops, shamelessly recounting Mike's passing and highlighting our desire to rebuild our shattered lives in a peaceful setting. The reply was prompt and double-edged: of the many applications received ours would be seriously considered. And so we waited…

Good omens

The owner named Michael (which we took to be a good omen) phoned to arrange a viewing, and on close examination every detail pleased and excited us. On the spot, I assured that affable farmer that we would be grateful, long term tenants. In our minds we'd already moved in and furnished each room, and as each day passed without further word the tension grew. Thus I ramped up our campaign and wrote a second pleading letter, this time cheekily enclosing a cheque to cover the first month's rent. Although Michael acknowledged the letter and enclosure, still no decision was forthcoming. As more time passed and our anxiety increased, the girls badgered me into phoning to ask if a decision had yet been made. I was loathe to pester the man but decided the benefits of taking the direct approach far outweighed the suspense. And joy of joys, the following day he phoned with the news we'd been hoping for. We started packing, adopted our first dog, Tessa, and moved in before summer's end.

Once again the girls started at new schools - senior public for Angi and high school for Amanda. I was pleased that Amanda seemed to have settled in this time, freeing me up to explore our new surroundings. Together with Tessa - soon sadly replaced by an adorable black Lab, called Jessa, who we adopted after Tessa met an untimely end one night at the end of our driveway - I forged new paths in behind the house and picked out secret spots beside the creek that lazily wound its way through the bush.

Understanding grief

I joined the library and borrowed books on bereavement, so hungry was I for knowledge to help deal with the heavy burden of grief I carried with me. I read accounts of bereaved parents' trials and tribulations and began to understand the theory behind the so-called stages of grief. Because my university days weren't all that far behind me and for so long I'd been in the habit of making notes, I found myself chronicling points relevant to my situation; all this I did in a desperate attempt to make sense of my increasingly dark world. By then I had made one friend, Michaela, our landlord's daughter, with whom I shared the first few chapters. She enthused over my work and suggested I turn it into a column for the local newspaper. Initially I took her suggestion less than seriously, assuming her praise was simply a demonstration of her empathy. But as I continued to read and make more notes I took her advice, particularly as she had put in a good word with the editor who was a friend of hers.

I submitted five one-page pieces, the first of which, to my surprise and delight, made press two weeks later. My column was born! Subsequently a head shot of me was inserted at the top of the column along with details of my new venture - a bereavement counselling service. Soon I had amassed a handful of clients who were grateful to pay a small fee for the help I offered in the comfort of their own homes.

Meanwhile I had no problem keeping ahead of press deadlines, a challenge I thoroughly enjoyed; not only was I satisfying my creative urges but helping myself and others to navigate the bumpy and perilous path of grief.

Settled at last!

Soon life in our country home became our norm. The girls bought their first pony, named her Ally and broke her for riding. Another black Lab, named Epee, became part of our gang along with a colony of guinea pigs and various other rodents. As it turned out, Amanda was again unable to tolerate school in a formal setting and opted for home learning combined with a teacher's aide position with younger students at Angi's school. Together, the girls boarded the school bus each morning, leaving me alone with Jessa and Epee. Now I was free to wander, to ponder and to write.

Week 1
Introduction

The death of a loved one is an experience many of us will face during our lifetime. Whether the loss is of a parent, spouse, child or friend, our sadness and pain may seem insurmountable. The purpose of this column is to help bereaved people to cope with the feelings and emotions that accompany loss. Also, the information shared week-by-week might serve as a guide for those who are searching for ways to help a friend or family member in grief.

There are several factors that affect the way we cope with loss: the passing of time; the amount of available support; and an understanding of the phases through which we will pass on our grief journey. The adage that time heals is, in part, true. But there is much to be gained through knowledge - verbal and written accounts of others' experience with grief. This learning is one type of support; another is that offered by a friend or professional with both willingness and expertise to listen, empathise and lighten our load.

Individuals grieving a loss will experience a combination of emotions (anger, sadness, jealousy, guilt) each of varying intensity and duration and in no particular order. However, the commonalties of the grief process are basic and recognisable. It is my intent, therefore, to share some ideas which may help readers to navigate the new territory into which they have been thrust. The goal is to eventually emerge safe and whole and ready to face a new life - one that though undeniably changed holds great potential for growth, achievement and peace.

We will begin our examination of the grief process next week with an overview of the stages of grief.

Week 2
Stages of Grief

As you work through your grief you will pass through stages - shock and denial, anger and depression - and finally reach a degree of acceptance. We will examine each stage in detail, but for the benefit of those who have already begun their grief journeys, I offer a brief overview.

We first find ourselves in denial, refusing to believe that our loved one has died. Our inability to face the truth is normal while our minds and bodies are in shock. Emotions run riot, and periods of panic, anger and sadness are interspersed with intervals of apparent calm due to our natural protective defences. As time passes and our defences begin to let down, we begin our search for reasons for our loss. Unable, however, to find answers, we become angry and look for something or someone on which to blame the death. Some direct anger at things or others they feel are responsible. Or God. Or, as illogical as it may seem, on the one who has died. We might also direct anger inwards in the form of guilt.

Anger for which there is no outlet morphs into depression. In this stage we are apathetic. Nothing matters, and our main task is to find the energy to simply get through each day. But even in sleep, we may still feel pain through dreams.

Each of these stages will repeat in random order. The sense that we are coping with our loss may come and go when, for instance, anniversary dates and certain songs or pictures trigger emotions with which we felt we had already dealt.

These stages as I have painted them may appear to be endless periods of discomfort and heartache. But I urge you to take courage as there will be times when you will feel comforting, uplifting emotions. And just as we must give ourselves permission to experience sadness and anger, so we must take advantage of feelings such as hope, peace and even joy when they present themselves.

Remember... confusing, changing emotions are normal reactions to loss. Next week we will take a close look at shock and denial.

Week 3
Shock and Denial

Whether a death is unexpected or a predictable ending to a long illness, the first reaction of those left behind is denial. In the case of accidental death or sudden physiological failure, one's inability to face reality is understandable. In any event, the finality of death is hard to grasp.

As we work through the funeral arrangements and legal and financial matters, logically we know the truth. But the emotional part of us, which yearns for our loved one to be alive, overrides logic and keeps the truth at bay. The death may seem like a bad dream from which we hope soon to awaken. While in this state of shock we need time to integrate the conflicting messages of head and heart. For this reason, the bereaved person may seem to be doing quite well, and onlookers might express surprise and even relief at the seemingly calm and controlled demeanour of the mourner.

It is important for family and friends to realise that when the numbness of shock first gives way to reality, the bereaved person will need help. During the quiet days after the funeral our body's protective defence mechanisms begin to relax. Grief attacks may occur during which fits of crying, despair and loneliness consume the griever. Other symptoms are confusion, lack of concentration and a perception of going crazy. Sleeping and eating patterns may be disrupted. Energy and motivation are at a low ebb, and tasks such as writing thank you notes and sorting through clothes and possessions may seem impossible to face alone.

The duration of this stage depends largely on the amount and type of support available. Thus it is important that we gain a basic understanding of the grief process so that, when called upon, we might confidently and effectively take on the role of support person. Next week we will look at specific ways that a concerned family member or friend might help.

Week 4
Role of Support Person

When the funeral is over, friends naturally return to their own families and busy schedules often with a reminder to "call if you need anything." But feeling tired and confused, the bereaved may give out a message that they will be alright and just need to be alone to reorganise their lives. But the truth is that grievers may not know what they want or need.

While bereaved people need a certain amount of quiet time, prolonged periods of silence and aloneness could compound feelings of desperation and loss. They may not phone the friend out of fear of becoming a nuisance or perhaps because they think they must somehow be strong enough to face their grief alone.

What bereaved people need most, however, is the chance to talk when they are ready - to vent their constantly changing emotions. As such, it is the task of the support person to take the initiative to call or drop by for a cup of tea and chat, thereby giving the griever an opportunity to go over the details of the death, if he or she so wishes, to share precious memories of the deceased or, indeed, to raise any one of their many concerns. The support persons' words are far less important than their presence; just being there is a show of willingness to listen and a desire to lighten the load. Some people don't always need to talk. One man told me of a friend's visit shortly after the sudden death of his wife. No words were spoken; the two simply sat together, held hands and cried, leaving the grieving husband feeling better afterwards.

The key word in the grief process is permission - an unspoken message that the griever is allowed to set the tone and pace of his healing, whether it is to talk, to cry, to reminisce or to touch in silence. And when the friend leaves with a promise to call later, he need not worry about what he said or should have said for he has the satisfaction of knowing that he was there when needed. Our gifts of time and show of concern are the ultimate gifts of true friendship.

Week 5
Early Response to Friends in Grief

Visitation, at a funeral parlour or at home, gives us an opportunity to offer condolences to the family shortly after the death of their loved one. As we search for words of solace we could resort to clichés: "It must be a relief after all he's suffered." "What a blessing you have other children." "One day you'll be together again." "He wouldn't have wanted to live like that!"

While these sentiments may contain some truth, people in the numbing grip of this early stage of grief may not be ready to face such basic truths while they struggle to grasp what has happened and begin to deal with the loss. Our church minister approached my mother with a serene smile on his face within two hours of my sister's passing, voicing his belief that she was lucky to be in heaven and no longer plagued by worldly worries. Obviously neither my mother nor I shared his joy and felt angry. It was a long while before my mother was able to take the meaning of the words of that man of the cloth as they were intended. Incidentally, given my own belief system and philosophy of life, I never did.

Two words - simplicity and sincerity - are the keys to ensure that meetings during these first harrowing days, weeks and even months will be comforting to the mourner and rewarding to the visitor. As such, it is best to put philosophical thoughts aside and address more immediate facts and feelings. "I was so sorry to hear that she's died." "What an awful shock that must have been for you." "It's so hard to believe that he has gone." "What can I do to help?" Or how about a heartfelt, "How are you doing?" while holding hands or giving a hug?

Any of these verbal and physical responses tend to normalise the bereaved person's feelings of shock, sadness and disbelief; as well, the demonstration of shared feelings opens up channels of communication and allows for further expression of grief. There will be ample opportunity to philosophise over the issues of life and death further down the road.

Week 6
Reliving Precious Memories

It's Christmas day and all the family is there except for one. The same thing happens at Easter and Thanksgiving. As you remember the way these family gatherings used to be, your mind wanders. Sadness and loneliness, even in the company of family and friends, washes over you like a wave.

The strange thing is, though, that your lost loved one may not be mentioned, in which case you might wonder if others present remember or feel the sting of the empty chair. It is quite likely that they, too, are thinking of that missing person but refrain from giving voice to their thoughts for fear of upsetting you or putting a damper on the gathering. Paradoxically the opposite is true; more than anything you need to have your loved one spoken of and the lack of his physical presence acknowledged.

The way in which we deal with grief is changing for the better. The feeling used to be that to bring up the past was to get stuck in it. While it is true, in certain cases, that dwelling on memories could be counter productive to healing, we now know that speaking of departed loved ones and looking at pictures helps us to come to terms with our grief. The one thing of which we are fearful is that our loved one might be forgotten, and it is through sharing memories that we celebrate the precious life that once was.

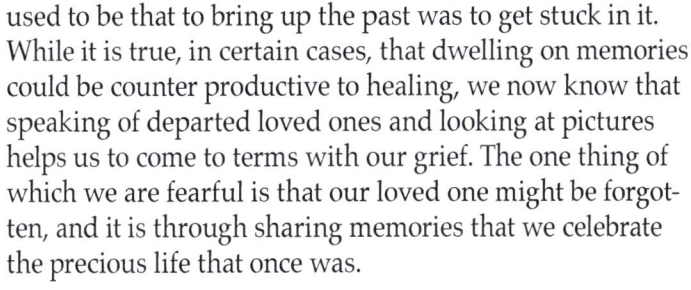

One way I handle special occasions is to put a candle close to my place at the table and, as I light it, say, "This is for Mike." This ritual brings me comfort and opens the door for others to join in and remember the good times. As we share memories and humorous anecdotes we might laugh or shed a tear. But no matter what emotions surface, their expression takes us one small step forward on our grief path.

Week 7
Crying as a Response to Grief

We often hear the expression, "Don't cry... it will be all right." When a child falls and scrapes his knee, we console him and urge him to stop crying, assuring him that a plaster and a sweet treat will take the pain away. Soon he is off playing, his tears and pain forgotten.

Crying is a normal part of the grief process and needs to be encouraged since it is one of nature's ways of releasing pain. Often after we cry we feel better because, along with our tears, our bodies release hormones that have a soothing effect on our entire system. Sometimes, then, we are able to relax and perhaps sleep. I picture the source of my tears as a pool deep inside me that fills with emotions as I strive to deal with my loss. If we fight back our tears our pool of sadness grows deeper and spills over, and the emotions bubbling throughout our bodies manifest in other ways. For this reason people in grief are prone to psychosomatic symptoms: difficulty swallowing or breathing; heart palpitations; digestive upsets; muscle tension and pain.

Therefore we must give ourselves and others permission to cry, and those taking a supportive role can help by reacting to tears in a positive way. When we notice tears welling up in a friend's eyes we need to be aware of our own body language. If we react with embarrassment or discomfort, lower our eyes, glance away or change the subject, we send a subtle but sure message that tears are not acceptable. The grieving person is then left to deal not only with the physical symptoms but also with the fear that crying is an inappropriate behaviour. In your role as a support person keep the tissues handy and be prepared to sit by patiently until the tears subside; when we cry we usually talk, and the more opportunities we have to speak about our loss the sooner we will come to peaceful resolution of the death.

Week 8
The Second Stage of Grief

I regard this period of grief, commonly called the anger stage, as the most difficult; no longer could I deny the fact that my son had died but as yet was unable to come to terms with the awful truth. During this painful time I experienced so many strong and changing emotions that I dubbed it the roller-coaster phase.

Undoubtedly anger is at the top of our list of emotions at this time and can flair up without warning - its source, our inability to justify the death. We can think of many reasons why our loved one should have lived but none for why she died. The 'if-onlys' dominate our thoughts as we think of the people and events we feel played a role in the outcome. "If only she hadn't taken that ride... had been diagnosed earlier... had stayed home that night... had been more careful... had talked to me about it." This type of thinking is normal and predictable and a temporary outlet and first step towards recognising and venting our anger.

Contrary to common belief, anger can be a positive emotion but with the potential to become negative when misdirected or uncontrolled. For this reason I caution against getting stuck in or compulsively acting upon the if-only's. I believe that our anger in grief is rooted in an overwhelming sense of powerlessness to turn back the clock and have things turn out differently - above all to have our loved one with us still. When we have exhausted all our sources of blame we may turn our anger towards life itself and question its fairness and worth.

In order to begin to heal we need to express our anger, and in future columns I will share some ideas on how we might do this. Once again I emphasise the importance of finding someone with whom we can freely share our feelings of frustration and anger. This person might be a friend or a professional.

Discussion groups offer opportunities to learn from those with experiences similar to our own. A group meeting might be just such a place.

Week 9
Bereavement Groups

Four months after my loss I attended my first meeting of a group specifically created for bereaved parents. Fifteen people at varying stages of grief were in attendance, and with the guidance of a leader we began with a check-in - a chance to introduce ourselves and briefly describe our losses and feelings. Since the leader continually reminded us that participation was voluntary, I found the atmosphere relaxing and non-threatening. Some parents gave detailed accounts of their experiences while others simply stated names and dates and passed the group's attention to the next person. Once we each had an opportunity to speak, the evening's topic, as agreed at a prior meeting, was introduced.

That evening's discussion centred around the Easter weekend just passed. We were invited to share our experiences and feelings during the holiday and ideas on how best to approach future family-focused gatherings. During check-out time the leader encouraged us to comment further to ensure that nobody left the meeting without receiving some crucial individual support.

On the drive home I felt more peaceful and hopeful than I had been since my son's death. As I recalled the discussion I realised that the group would serve three main purposes. First, the knowledge that all the attendees were in the same boat helped me to feel less alone. Secondly, the group environment was a safe one in which I could freely express emotions without fear of shocking others or being judged by them. Thirdly, I knew that through hearing others' experiences I, too, could learn to cope with my grief.

Groups are an excellent place to start the healing but not the only one. It may not be possible for some, for personal reasons or because of geography and transportation, to attend a formal gathering. But there are many other options to choose and combine to suit individual needs and preferences, two of which are reading and writing.

Week 10
Help Through Reading and Writing

Everyone has a personal concept of the grief journey; mine is that of clambering up a craggy mountain, working my way along the rocky paths and finally reaching its peak. From that vantage point I envision a clear view of the horizon and a readiness to descend the other side to rejoin the world. But first I needed to find the most direct paths on my ascent.

One of my tools is reading, and there is much to be learned from others' personal accounts. My local library proved to be an excellent resource. Some books I read cover to cover; others I scanned, reading only the chapters that seemed relevant to my feelings at the time. In any case my reading time was well spent, for the wisdom I gleaned increased my understanding of grief as a normal human process. So, too, I learned many coping strategies through the written word.

Writing is another helpful tool, and my journal has become the silent friend that helps me to identify and sort through my feelings. Anyone with basic skills can keep a journal since rules of grammar and spelling are less important than instinct and freedom to allow thoughts to surface. Start with one or two words and you may be amazed at the way they flow into sentences, paragraphs and then full pages. Sometimes journal writing turns into poetry - not necessarily the kind with rhythm and rhyme but of a style all our own. It is helpful to not only write but occasionally reread your journal as it offers valuable insights into how you are feeling and why. As well, your journal may become a log by which you chart your progress.

As I flip through the pages of my journal I note that many of the entries are written as if I was speaking directly to my son. I have discovered that directing thoughts and words to a lost loved one is a common practice and a healthy expression of the yearning that accompanies loss. Next week we will explore other ways through which this yearning may surface.

Week 11
Yearning and Preoccupation

During this roller-coaster ride there will be times of yearning so strong that we actually search for the person for whom we grieve, half-hoping or even expecting to see them. This can happen on visits to familiar places when vivid memories from the not-so-distant past leap into the present. The occurrence may be as simple as sitting in your living room and glancing at the empty chair, seeing the person, looking again and realising that the vision was a product of imagination. Such situations are more than wishful thinking; they are a temporary buffer and our mind's way of slowly coming to grips with reality.

I truly believe that silent conversations with loved ones are also normal expressions of yearning and need not be taken as signs of 'losing it'. On the contrary, when we communicate this way we are actually advancing along our grief path by expressing feelings and perhaps even resolving unfinished business.

Preoccupation with those who have died goes hand-in-hand with yearning as we resume our daily routines. Even a trip to the grocery store can be a challenge. As I walked down the aisles and filled my basket I could not help but think of my son's culinary likes and dislikes and his delight at coming home to the delicious aroma of his favourite meal. It was the same at McDonalds where he'd worked, the bus station and football games - so many sad thoughts in places I had formerly frequented with a light heart and relaxed step.

There is no magic formula for getting through this time and no time line to follow. The key to handling yearning and preoccupation lies in the knowledge that the flashbacks lessen in intensity and frequency as time passes. And because each of us is unique, we must resist the temptation to compare our progress with that of others.

There are many factors that affect individual reactions to loss. Next week we will begin an examination of the grief journey with respect to these factors.

Week 12
Factors Affecting our Grief Response

Many aspects of life affect our reaction to loss through death and lead us along varying paths on our grief journeys. Two major factors are the actual circumstances of the death and our perception of its preventability.

Generally speaking, the circumstances of the death, including its suddenness and nature, have a direct bearing on the amount of time we may expect to spend in a state of shock and disbelief. In the case of accidental death when our only warning may be a call from the hospital or police, we have precious little lead time to emotionally prepare for our loss, as we have when death is predictable following a prolonged illness. Often after an untimely visit from the grim reaper, shock and disbelief may be magnified through a lack of knowledge of the events that led to the death. If this is the case, one goal of grief work is to accept the fact that we may never make sense of the details or find all the answers. Some grievers dwell on the question of the pain that they imagine their loved ones may have suffered. As questions arise, however, it is important that they are aired, discussed and, if not answered fully, eventually put to rest.

Our reaction to death, both accidental or expected, also depends on our perceptions as to whether or not it could have been prevented. As with the question around pain and suffering, we could drive ourselves to distraction by playing and replaying our mental tapes, each time changing one minute detail to alter the outcome. While this type of thinking may seem magical and non-productive to an onlooker, it does serve one important purpose; over time we come to the conclusion that a number of factors, many or all out of our control, came together to precipitate the death. At the same time, as we allow our thoughts to wander and recreate scenes in our minds, we begin to recognise and release our anger over the loss.

Both of these factors must be taken into consideration as they apply to our own grief scenarios. Next week we will look at what is felt to be the prime factor in our grief reaction - the uniqueness and closeness of our relationship with the deceased.

Week 13
Uniqueness of Relationship

While the following example may, at first glance, seem inappropriate when speaking of human life and death, it demonstrates in simple terms the link between closeness and reaction to loss.

Last spring my daughters found a tiny living creature, as yet hairless and pink. We named her Soupy, a shortened version of what we guessed her to be - a marsupial. For two weeks she wriggled and crawled blindly inside a box warmed with a heating pad. Each morning the girls awoke to Soupy's hungry squeaks, and in their absence it fell upon me to feed her warm milk from a medicine dropper.

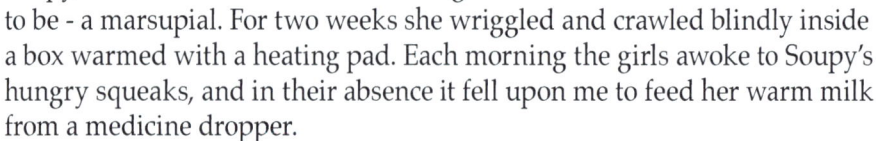

One sad day she did not wake up; we presumed the culprit to be a too-high heat setting. For whatever reason Soupy was dead, and we felt sad and angry as we buried our little friend. We had bonded with that tiny vulnerable creature, cared for her as best we could and looked forward to watching her grow. Had she died before we'd found her in the grass there would have been no relationship, hence no sadness or anger at her premature departure.

So it is with those we love and lose. The closer the attachment the more deeply we react to loss. We miss all those parts of the relationship that made it so special. That person who we perhaps lived with, cared for, and with whom we shared hopes and dreams has gone. Grief is an acknowledgement of love, and the nature of our relationship with that person is reflected in its depth. For this reason, as well as for the fact that grief is a unique process, we must resist the temptation to urge others to follow our exact paths. Although we might identify with others' feelings, we must give credence to the fact that their relationship was theirs alone.

When we lose a loved one, absence of presence is only one of the effects. Next week we will look at secondary losses and role changes that inevitably accompany loss.

Week 14
Recognizing Secondary Losses

There are an infinite number of ways in which we experience loss, and secondary losses follow as a natural consequence to the loss of physical presence. For those who are widowed, the loss may trigger significant role changes. Routine daily tasks such as shopping and cooking and cleaning, previously the responsibility of the one who has died, may present as major obstacles. Likewise for those whose mates took care of the family financial matters, keeping up with banking and bill payment may compound feelings of confusion, anger and frustration that are normal reactions to grief. The problem, as well, is that when we assume new duties we feel our loss all the more deeply for they are constant reminders of the many ways in which we miss our loved one. A reminder for me was a computer problem for which my son always had a solution. I now must turn to other sources for technical help.

A diminished social life can be a substantial loss for the newly widowed. Community dances, country fairs and church functions are activities that take on a different flavour for those who always attended as a couple. Thus the bereaved person may choose to stay at home rather than face situations which serve to compound their sense of isolation. But staying at home may not be the best solution either for it is in those quiet, familiar surroundings that painful memories are triggered. And if mobility is an issue and the remaining partner cannot drive, the sense of isolation may be frighteningly real.

Those who are embarking on their grief journeys may find this short list of secondary losses long and ominous, but I bring these points to your attention because I believe that to be forewarned is to be forearmed. You will probably not experience all of these losses, and the intensity of those with which you identify will lessen over time. Remember, too, that with patience, perseverance and a healthy dose of self-compassion, you will learn new skills and incorporate them into your new lifestyle.

Being good to yourself includes asking for help from friends, family and community members. Another healthy technique involves putting on your comfort coat - the topic of next week's column.

Week 15
Putting on our Comfort Coats

Anyone who has grieved will agree that there are good days, when we feel capable of coping, and bad days that bring us back to what feels like square one. As time passes, however, the good days begin to outnumber the bad - a change which, I believe, is in direct relation to attainment of coping strategies.

One mother described her practice of taking a few quiet moments early in the day to hug one of her son's favourite stuffed toys. While this routine likely conjured up memories that brought tears, the animal became her way to connect with her son. This association is a necessary part of the healing process since one of our fears is that our loved one might drift so far from our consciousness as to fade away. When we take time to don our comfort coats, we acknowledge our loss and psychically touch the life that once was. Each morning I routinely pick up my son's stuffed monkey; as I hug Monk I satisfy my need to connect with Mike and thus put myself in a more peaceful frame of mind.

Each of our many comfort coats differs according to our personalities and preferences. I wear one of mine when I walk in nature. As I take note of seasonal changes around me - tiny green shoots in spring and crisp, colourful leaves each autumn - I cannot help but accept the inevitability of change and regrowth as revealed in nature's life cycle.

Many people find comfort through spirituality and religion, scripture and worship. Some find a modicum of peace within the home in such simple tasks as baking, preparing a favourite meal or sewing some new cushions. A bubble bath can be a relaxing refuge - a place to quietly gather our thoughts before we head off to bed with a cup of cocoa and a good book. Hobbies too, though often temporarily abandoned during the early stages of grief, are a good source of relaxation and satisfaction. Whether your comfort coat puts you in closer touch with your loved one or offers a welcome diversion, it is important that you persevere and try on several coats until you find one or more which best suit you.

Next week we turn our attention to the Christmas season - a time when newly-bereaved people need all the comfort and help they can get.

Week 16
Planning for Christmas

The Christmas season is a time of family gatherings, cards, gifts, carols and elaborate meals. But for those who have lost a loved one during the year, this season is sure to bring mixed emotions. And because Christmas is a family time it is important that members of bereaved families plan the season's activities in advance in order to meet individual needs. Often this means a deviation from long-standing family traditions.

As our first Christmas without Mike loomed close, his sisters and I planned some small but beneficial changes. I felt that digging out the familiar ornaments and decorating a tree would evoke painful memories with which I, personally, was not yet ready to deal. On the other hand, the girls saw the tree as an important part of their Christmas; and so it was decided that they would be responsible for setting up and decorating the tree.

Shopping for gifts was another task I knew would take more emotional and physical energy than I was willing to expend. Together we drew up a simple gift list for which the girls could easily shop. These two solutions worked well for us; they relieved me of some responsibility and gave Mike's young siblings freedom to get into the spirit of the season.

This freedom to make changes extends into all facets of the holiday season. Friends will understand if you decide against sending Christmas cards or taking part in the cookie exchange. You might choose to attend an earlier church service rather than the traditional midnight candlelight mass. It may be necessary to ask another family member to organise and cook Christmas dinner; or perhaps you may all decide to go out for the meal instead. Our Christmas dinner that first year was a homemade pizza - a necessary break from tradition and its preparation a welcome diversion and fun time.

The bottom line in getting through the Christmas season when we are grieving is accepting our limitations and communicating our needs and wishes to others. Next week we will look at more ways to cope with Christmas and specifically, invitations.

Week 17
Invitations and Social Gatherings

As Christmas approaches family members and friends extend invitations to bereaved people in the hope of helping them through this particularly difficult time. But as a newly bereaved person you may wonder how these visits will be and perhaps be tempted to decline invitations rather than deal with the uncertainty of the emotions that may surface. However tempting it may seem to shut yourself away until the festivities are over, it is probably best to make the effort to mingle, at least for part of the holiday. And there are ways to accept offers of hospitality that will reduce the pressure of making decisions. You might say, "Thanks for inviting me. I'd like to join you, and I know you'll understand if later on I should decide I can't come." And once there you can hang onto the secure thought that, should you feel too uncomfortable to stay, your friends will understand if you excuse yourself from the gathering.

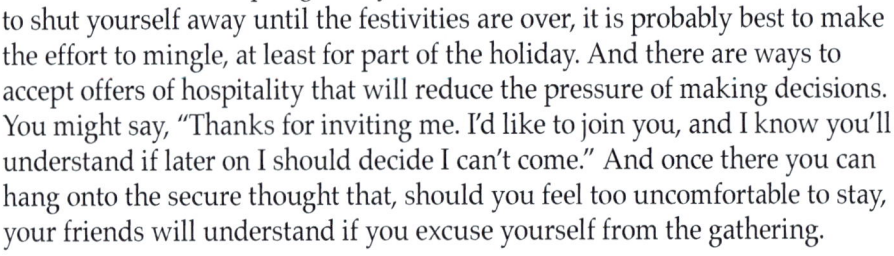

Many grieving people are surprisingly strong on special occasions because our natural defences prepare and protect us during difficult times. In fact, you may find that Christmas day passes a lot easier than you had thought, but don't be surprised if a day or two later you find yourself in the grip of a grief attack. I felt a sense of relief on the evening of the first anniversary of my son's death and even congratulated myself on how well I had got through the day. However, when I awoke feeling sad and distressed I realised I was having the predictable deferred grief response of which I'd been warned. This delayed reaction is normal as our defences let down, and we need to remember that sooner or later our grief will hit us head on!

I recently spent some time with a woman whose son had died two years earlier. She was experiencing physical symptoms resulting from repression of her feelings but had yet to allow herself the freedom to deal with her grief. Her healing began by first acknowledging her loss and then by identifying symbols which she could use as tools to help her to heal.

Week 18
Coping and Healing through Symbolism

Research on the grieving process reveals that communicating with others in like circumstances is of immeasurable value. Soon after our loss my girls and I linked up with Bereaved Families of Ontario, an organisation established to help in the event of the death of a child. We attended an information evening one month before Christmas; the focus of the discussion was the use of symbolism in grief.

We can use symbols as coping aids. For example, we make a donation to Bereaved Families by buying an angel for their Christmas tree. The emotional return is two-fold; we support a worthy cause and most importantly give a gift in the name and memory of our son and brother.

One mother spoke of the hour or two she spends on Christmas Eve, alone in the quiet darkness except for one candle that she lights as a symbol of her daughter's presence. This yearly ritual is not a morbid experience; rather it is a very real way to get in touch with feelings that inevitably surface at special family times. Some people donate a gift to a local agency, to be distributed to needy children. The symbolism here is that although we cannot give gifts to the ones who are no longer with us, we have the satisfaction that comes from giving to another in their memory.

Visiting the grave or the spot where ashes were scattered, and lighting a candle in a church, are ways to symbolically connect with lost loved ones. Although we cannot deny the fact that these rituals fall far short of what we really wish we could do at Christmas, over time they can become an accepted and meaningful ritual at certain times of the year.

If you are facing a first or even second Christmas without a family member, take heart and summon courage. Talk with those who you think might be of help. Share your feelings and misgivings, and identify symbols that you might use within your family circle.

Next week we will resume our examination of the factors that affect our grief response.

Week 19
Multiple and Prior Losses

Another factor to be considered in grief work is the number of former losses we have faced and the way in which we coped. This is not to imply that our grief journey through subsequent losses is any easier - quite the contrary in fact, for residual emotions from past loss have a way of resurfacing and complicating the issues of a more recent one.

Often the time that has elapsed between losses has little bearing on the type of grief reaction we might experience. One man reacted strongly to the death of his cousin, with whom he'd had little contact over the years, to the degree that his wife was surprised and alarmed at the depth of his sorrow. This man's reaction was quite normal. His mother died when he was young and at a time when the effects of grief were misunderstood and little or no help was available. As he mourned his cousin, this man was dealing with repressed emotions and memories of his mother and her death. Eventually he sought professional help and was able to deal with his emotions of the past and separate them from those of the present.

When we experience multiple deaths over a short period of time, we may suffer from grief overload, in which case we need to be even more patient with ourselves than in the event of a single loss. Our grief process may be more complicated, our emotions more changeable and recovery time longer. In such cases I would recommend that professional help be sought.

Yet another factor, apart from experience, is personality and temperament. Some people seem better able to cope with loss than others. There is no explanation for the wide range of reactions other than an acknowledgement of one's individuality. It bears repeating that because of our uniqueness we must consider all aspects of ourselves and circumstances as we travel our grief path and assess our progress.

Week 20
Age and Life Fulfillment Factors of Loss

Reactions vary according to the age of our lost loved one and our perception of their fulfilment of life. It has been said that to lose a parent is to lose one's past; to lose a mate is to lose one's present; and to lose a child is to lose one's future. When a child or a person in the prime of life is taken from us, we not only mourn the relationship we have lost but equally focus on the lost potential of life. This loss of future is double-edged; we who survive, particularly parents, are left with a multitude of broken dreams. This reaction may seem to be a selfish one, but it is perfectly natural considering that when our children are born we plan our lives around a future with them. The other edge of the sword is that we feel sad and angry on behalf of our young loved one who was deprived of his or her future.

Many of our emotions arise from our perception of unfinished business that may be viewed in different but equally significant ways. We might dwell on plans that our loved one had made - a university degree, a business venture, travel, marriage and family. Any unfinished business between ourselves and our loved ones may also present us with additional stress and heightened emotions. We may second-guess many aspects of our relationships and harbour feelings of regret and guilt over things said or left unsaid, done or left undone. These thoughts and issues need to be addressed as we work our way towards a sense of peaceful closure.

Over the past weeks I have offered a brief overview of the main factors that affect our grief reactions with the purpose of helping readers to assess their responses. With this information you might make a mental check list of the factors as they apply to your situation and thereby gain a better understanding of yourself and your journey. This list can be used as a measure of the work necessary to reach your mountain's peak and a gauge by which to pace yourself.

Week 21
Physiological Concerns

When we are physically ill we might note a change in our state of mind in the form of worry, anxiety and depression. The opposite holds true in that our physical health can be affected when we go through an emotional upheaval. Bereaved people need to acknowledge the link between their psychological and physiological selves and take steps to maintain a reasonable level of physical health.

A change in sleep patterns is a common complaint. Difficulty falling asleep and waking early or during the night is indicative of a troubled mind. The problem with sleep deprivation is that neither our minds nor our bodies get sufficient rest, without which we lack the bodily and emotional strength to face the tasks associated with grieving and healing.

To counteract fatigue and lower our body's susceptibility to viruses, infections and disease, we need to make a conscious effort to rest. Catnaps during the day are one solution to catching up on sleep, or we may resort to traditional methods to induce drowsiness - a warm bath, soft music, a gentle television program or a good book.

Drugs bring temporary relief and, if prescribed by a doctor, serve their purpose in the short term. Alcohol may have the same effect, but prolonged use of either of these may be harmful to health and counter-productive to emotional healing. Dulled minds and artificially controlled emotions could indefinitely postpone grief work. And as we begin to work through our feelings once friends have gone back to their routines, loneliness could lead to substance dependency.

Our appetites may change, and we might skip meals or choose foods that fail to provide our bodies with the necessary nutrition. Weight loss is common but usually short-lived if we make an effort to balance our diet once we begin to feel more stable.

Exercise has obvious physical benefits; it helps to overcome sleep problems and is an excellent outlet for anger and depression. Next week we will look at exercising and other ways of releasing emotion.

Week 22
Staying Healthy and Venting Anger

How strange it would be to lose an important person in our lives and bounce right back, apparently the same as we were before! To do so would be to deny the drastic change that our world has undergone. It is equally absurd to deny the emotions that surface through grief, one of which is anger. We may find it difficult to express anger or reluctant to admit to having what is commonly but mistakenly felt to be a negative emotion.

Exercise is therapy for body and soul and an excellent outlet for anger. The physical benefits are well known. After a brisk walk, a home workout, fitness class, game of tennis or bowling - any activity in which we use muscles, raise our heart rate and increase blood flow - we feel more relaxed, and the psychological benefits are three-fold. While we concentrate on physical activity, we temporarily defocus from our grief. Secondly, we feel good about ourselves simply by knowing that we are making the effort to care for our bodies. Thirdly, as we expend physical energy we release nervous energy. I once played a game of tennis as a way to vent my anger; having forewarned my opponent of my state of mind, I hit the ball as hard as I could. When the game was over I felt tired but relieved.

Just as exercise is an emotional release so are certain causes we may choose to take on. One parent working through her grief derived satisfaction by establishing MADD (Mothers Against Drunk Drivers). The British Columbia dad, whose daughter was murdered, travelled across Canada to raise support for a change in parole laws. These people re-channelled the energy they invested in the relationship with their loved one, and we each need to search for the right channels. One of mine is educating others as to the dangers of playing hyperventilation games. Two more are writing and counselling. Volunteering is yet another worthwhile way to expend time and energy.

By turning anger into action we begin to take charge of our lives and move further along our grief path. By contrast, repressed anger can turn into depression, next week's topic.

Week 23
Reactive Depression

No matter how committed we are to working through our anger, this phase of the grief process is usually followed by, or intermingled with, periods of reactive depression. Some symptoms are sadness, apathy, helplessness, loneliness, difficulty concentrating and making decisions, crying, irritability, low self-esteem and fatigue. Many of these symptoms parallel those of a clinical depression, but there is a difference. By recognising the source of reactive depression, such as a death, we can take heart in the knowledge that our symptoms will decrease in number and intensity as we work through our grief.

We do not always recognise our symptoms or adequately describe our feelings to a friend or professional in words that will alert them to our depressive state. All we may know is that we feel differently now, and it is often through changes in our behaviour that depression is diagnosed. A change in dress or appearance from neat to unkempt is a clue. Another sign is irritability when once we were agreeable. Depression has been described as anger turned inward, and our irritability may stem from anger at ourselves for the part we think we played in the loss or our perceived inability to cope.

Bereaved people need time alone to adjust to changes, but prolonged social withdrawal is a warning to seek help. Depression is unique in that it is cyclical. Lethargy leads to a lack of motivation to engage in activities that might lift our spirits, and lowered activity feeds into feelings of helplessness and loneliness. A simple example of this cycle is a reluctance to get out of bed. But if we manage to muster the energy to get dressed, take a walk or pick up the mail, we give ourselves a chance, albeit brief, to think of something other than our loss. Along the way we may find someone to talk to, and once we have made contact with the outside world we have made a small but important break in the cycle of depression.

Depression is a normal consequence of grief, and the keys are patience and perseverance. By recognising the symptoms, asking for and accepting help when offered and taking small steps, we can work our way up and out of depression.

Week 24
The Burden of Guilt

As we question the whys and wherefores of loss, the *if onlys* have potential to add to the weight of guilt. One obvious source that comes to mind is a feeling that we may have contributed to the death or at the very least failed to prevent it. To make matters worse, our mixed, changeable emotions fuel the fire of guilt. One woman shared with me her desire to put her deceased husband on a pedestal but at the same time felt remorse over her relief that some of the more difficult aspects of her marriage had ended. By accepting the reality that no relationship, or human being, is perfect, she dropped her guilt and focused on more positive memories.

Feelings of guilt often arise when we remember times with our loved one that we would change if given the chance. As we work to resolve this unfinished business, we let ourselves off the hook by accepting the inevitable; the past is unchangeable but can be reframed into a more positive picture.

The sense of relief we feel following death after a lengthy illness may cause ambivalence and trigger guilt. The long and painful days and weeks are over, and we are thankful that the suffering has finally ended. In this case, the integration of conflicting emotions of relief and guilt is often a difficult task.

Anger goes hand-in-hand with guilt when we displace anger onto an innocent party - a common occurrence in grief. We may question our reactions and turn our regrets into guilt.

The anger/guilt connection may become an issue when we attempt but fail to keep our anger under control. Emotions such as sadness and yearning seem acceptable but anger inappropriate. Therefore an expression of anger could give rise to guilt.

Another source of guilt is our inability to justify our continuing earthly existence after a partner or a child dies. This survivor guilt is often a factor in a parent's or sibling's grief.

Guilt crops up in so many situations that it could become a serious obstacle to our healing process. I have briefly described some of the circumstances in which we formalise guilt feelings. Next week we will look at healthy ways of ridding ourselves of guilt.

Week 25
What about Guilt?

All emotions are legitimate by virtue of the fact that we do not invite them. Sadness arises out of yearning and anger out of frustration over things that happen out of our control. But in grief, guilt does not have any such legitimacy and serves no useful purpose.

To rid ourselves of guilt we first must acknowledge our feelings. We can do this by talking, because chances are that the words guilt or self-blame will come up in conversation. The next point to remember is that guilt is a self-inflicted emotion; when we are confused, we may interpret life's circumstances in too personal a way.

Hindsight is always twenty-twenty! How perfect life would be if we had such vision. The reality is, however, that we all make mistakes and do not have the luxury of total control of our lives and those of others. The key to dropping guilt is forgiving ourselves for our humanness. Forgiveness must not be confused with forgetting; it is not possible or even necessary to forget events in our past that cause self-doubt. But we can forgive ourselves, and I offer the following example shared by grief consultant and colleague, Dr. Bill Webster.

Imagine a reversal of roles: your loved one is alive and you have passed over. Would you want him or her to suffer the torment of guilt? Or would your message be, "Don't fret. I'd rather you remember all the wonderful things you did for me!"

If you try this exercise you may be surprised to find that you can forgive yourself as you know your loved one would. It may be helpful, too, to make a list of all the special times that you shared, using photographs as graphic reminders. And if you still feel twinges of guilt, you may dispel them by realising that you did what you could at the time, which is all that any of us can do. Keep in mind, too, that the grief process is unique and that you need time to reach that happy state of self-forgiveness. You will know you are successful when you feel the peace that accompanies a cleared conscience.

A lot of the grief work I have talked about thus far describes what is known as our grief reaction. Now it is time to move on to look at our grief responses, and next week we will flush out the subtle yet important differences.

Week 26
Reaction vs. Response

Over the past weeks I have shared information that might broaden your understanding of the grief process and used the word reaction in describing the many facets of each stage. A summary of the information reads as follows:

Grief is very real. It is painful, and so it hurts. We react to pain through our emotions. And at any point during the grief process, perhaps our one comforting thought comes from knowing that our reactions are normal.

I have talked about climbing mountains, travelling along paths and getting on with the rest of our lives. To accomplish this monumental task we need to do more than accept our reactions. For inasmuch as we must give ourselves permission to react, our individual response to loss directly affects the duration and outcome of our grief journeys. Thus, after we have allowed ourselves sufficient time to react to our new situations, we must move on to a phase in which we make an effort to take responsibility for our healing - to respond appropriately. We begin to make decisions and choose constructive ways of dealing with grief - for example, putting on our comfort coats - bearing in mind that we are hurting and with good reason.

The steps we take are personal, and there is no right or wrong way to respond. The only rule is that we do respond, each in our own way. It may be a trial-and-error approach, especially if this is our first encounter with death, and we might follow others' examples to find ways to help ourselves. The point, though, is that we purposely pursue different avenues and activities to facilitate our healing, and we successfully respond by persevering until we find our own best ways.

I believe that in any life situation communication is the cornerstone to healing and growth. Human beings are social creatures and, as such, need to trust that we may turn to one another in times of need. By talking through our feelings, we take a big first step and an active approach to grief - a perfect example of a healthy response.

"Give sorrow words; the grief that does not speak whispers the o'er-fraught heart, and bids it break." Shakespeare, Macbeth

Week 27
Grief Attacks

Slowly we begin to put our lives back together. I have spoken with bereaved people who returned to their jobs within weeks of their loss. Some reported finding comfort in familiar surroundings where they could focus their thoughts outward on their tasks rather than inward on their pain. Others, given the option, took a leave of absence and returned to work when they felt better able to face the workaday world. Either way, at home or at work, we must be prepared for grief attacks - periods when the pain of loss suddenly overwhelms us.

Dr. Webster coined the phrase 'grief attack', an apt description of the grip of pain and the spilling over of emotions, usually through tears. He likens the experience to watching waves roll onto the shore. In grief, waves of sadness wash over us often when we least expect them. They may be triggered by a chance meeting with a friend, a telephone conversation, a song, smell or place. It is the element of surprise that makes us all the more vulnerable to grief attacks; just as some waves are bigger and hit the shore with more force than others, grief attacks vary in frequency and intensity.

The way in which we handle grief attacks depends on the immediate situation and our individual response to grief. In some circumstances an expression of feelings on the spot is appropriate; at other times a retreat to a private place for the length of time it takes to release tears feels right. The important point to remember is that we need not feel embarrassed by grief attacks and should let them run their course. At certain times it may be best to grit our teeth and fight back our tears momentarily, but if we continually side-step our grief, sooner or later our pool of emotions will find another, perhaps more debilitating outlet. Grief attacks are healthy signs that we are working through our grief towards the day when the attacks will become all but memories.

Next week we will look at the final phase of grief work.

Week 28
Acceptance

There are many aspects of grieving to be covered in weeks to come, but for now it might be beneficial to look towards our goal and examine the final stage of grief. Those who are moving back and forth between shock, anger and depression may wonder when and how they might ever reach that coveted point; during the early days, I refused to even read about this phase much less imagine myself reaching it. I see now that this refusal came from my intense desire to deny the truth. How could I look ahead to accepting a death that I still worked so hard to deny?

Progress through grief is slow but sure. During bad times we tend to believe that our grief attacks are as intense and our depression as deep as when we began our journey. We may feel hopelessly stuck, but the reality is that we have simply reached a plateau on our mountain. What we need do during these times is simply trust that around the next bend there is hope: that we'll make it; that life can be meaningful once more; that we'll laugh and feel joy again. The strength of our hope is directly related to the effort we put into facing and dealing with our grief. We may draw on this mysterious ingredient called hope and regard each new challenge not as a stumbling block but a stepping stone and a test of our strength and faith.

Then one day we surprise ourselves. We begin to make plans, to look forward to an event or to make a major decision that might give our lives new meaning. It is then that we know we have weathered the worst. We can still expect to hit rough patches but they, too, will pass. This is the beginning of acceptance. In all likelihood it will never feel right that our loved one has died. It simply cannot be so. The best I can do is accept the fact that my son died because I have no choice but to do otherwise.

Time alone does not heal. Rather, we heal over time as we make choices and find new meaning for our lives. One major change may be in our philosophy of life, religious beliefs and spirituality. These topics will be addressed next week.

Week 29
Spirituality and Religion

As already mentioned, symbolism plays an important role in the grief process. As well as picturing myself climbing a mountain and following certain paths, I envision my moods and feelings as a pendulum swinging back and forth between extremes. So quickly, it seems, our positive feelings can change to those of desperation, especially when we are in the throes of a grief attack.

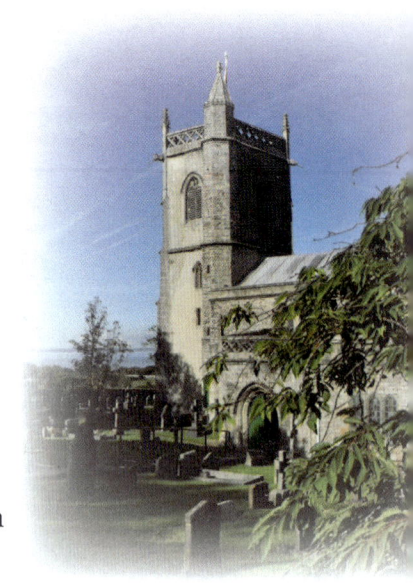

This swinging pendulum image might also be useful in understanding changes in religious and spiritual thinking and behaviours. As we focus on the unfairness of life and search for answers, our beliefs and faith may swing far left or right. Church attendance, worship and prayer might become an even greater part of life. Others, for many reasons one of which may be anger, debunk traditional forms of worship and seek alternative routes to satisfy their spiritual needs. Some find comfort in attending services of different religious denominations while others may put their spiritual lives on hold. Some behaviours may seem totally out of character, especially if that person worshipped regularly before the loss; they may be taking a temporary leave of absence - a time out - until they feel strong enough to deal with the emotions that could possibly surface in church so soon after the funeral.

Everyone handles grief differently but the pain is the griever's and so, therefore, are our choices. If you are recently bereaved or are supporting another who has lost a loved one, remember the swinging pendulum. Go along with your choices and changes, and respect those of others. The chances are that the pendulum will swing back to a central point and religious beliefs and practices return to normal. But if not, we need to accept the changes as a new but valid part of ourselves, family members and friends.

Next week's topic is philosophy of life - another perspective that may change drastically after a death.

Week 30
Philosophy of Life

When one we love dies it is as if a line has been drawn through our lives. I find that I now speak in terms of before and after Mike's death. Outwardly we may seem much the same as before, and friends breathe a sigh of relief when we appear to have returned to normal. However, a close death affects us to the core - so much so that we are profoundly changed. Hence, many bereaved people develop a different way of looking at the world and a new philosophy of life.

This cognitive switch is a subtle process born of our search for answers and an intense need to find new meaning. One obvious sign of my change was my reaction to trivial concerns, which before the loss were of major importance. Now, however, trivia seems inconsequential when viewed in the larger context of life and death.

Although everyday trivialities must be dealt with, some aspects of life take on new meaning. My relationship with my remaining children took precedence over a squeaky-clean house. In fact, a large part of my whole family's change process was a re-evaluation of our lifestyle and a focusing on dreams, leading to our move from the city to a smaller community, a country home, open fields and quiet wooded trails.

While some consider it unwise to make major changes soon after a loss, our changing thought patterns and beliefs invariably lead us in new directions. The certain knowledge of our mortality gives us the impetus to differentiate between what is important and what is not - to list and prioritise new goals and invest energy into realising them.

Change is part of life and brings with it losses and gains. We do not choose to have death touch our lives but, as we approach the final phase of grief, we may find the experience to be an opportunity for personal growth. I urge you, therefore, to give your revelations about life credibility as they have the potential to take you along a new life path filled with meaning, promise and peace.

Week 31
Parting with Possessions

Just as many factors influence our reactions to loss so it is when we address the question of when and how to part with clothing and possessions. I have spoken with people who immediately set about accomplishing the task and others who felt more comfortable tackling the job after some time had passed.

As with other issues of grief, there is no right or wrong way to deal with possessions. If you feel it's time to begin the sorting but lack motivation, it may be that you need some help. Possibly a friend might work along with you to help make decisions on what to keep or dispose of. As you work together you will find yourself reliving precious memories and expressing emotions. And when the job is completed, you may feel a huge sense of relief and a feeling of moving on.

If, however, you are procrastinating over the sort-out and are upset about feeling unable to face it, the help you need may be of a more formal therapeutic nature. A trained professional can help you to see whether or not your reluctance to face the job is rooted in denial. This type of support will allow for discussion and help you to move through a difficult stage of your grief process. Once you have done this, you may feel ready to call upon a friend and get the sorting done.

Some people set aside a special place in their home for the most precious items. It could be a shelf in a china cabinet - a place to visit to connect with our loved one. We may decide to keep and use a favourite chair or footstool or to wear certain items of clothing. And as painful as it may seem to live with the reminders, eventually these items become sources of comfort that trigger memories of happy times past.

Week 32
Children in Mourning

As parents, we strive to do all we can to protect our children's health and happiness. And so it is when a close family member dies: our first impulse is to spare our children the pain that accompanies loss. Studies have shown, however, that a bereaved child will need help in confronting the death. The logic behind these findings is that, no matter what age, we must all deal with grief lest we carry the residual emotions far into our future.

When my sister died suddenly my nephew was four, and his father dealt with the loss of his young wife by burying the past. There was no talk of the absent mother and wife, and any reminders - her belongings and pictures - were packed away out of sight and apparently out of mind. That boy, now a man of thirty-three, recently wrote so eloquently: "It was as if someone had ripped the first five years from my photo album - as if my life began at five when dad remarried. I wish I could get those years back."

Eventually he delved into his past, spoke with extended family members and retrieved memories of his mum and the lost years. Having accomplished this difficult task he put to rest many of the ghosts of his past.

Unresolved grief can lead to adult psychosomatic and conduct disorders, depression and neuroses. Thankfully, now, we are beginning to understand the long term effects of early loss and know that by adopting an educated, active approach to helping children deal with their feelings, we are protecting them in the long run.

In making what may seem to be a dark prognosis, I do not mean to be an alarmist. There are many ways in which we can guide our children safely through the grief process so that they emerge from childhood emotionally sound and equipped to face their happy tomorrows.

Week 33
When Baby Loses Mum

Much of the grief research on babies and young children is based on the death of the mother, since she is the person most likely to be the infant's main caregiver. However, the wisdom that applies to a mother's death can be generalised to others.

Infants in the first three months of life react to loss by crying and showing distress, but once their basic needs (food, warmth, comfort, touch) are met by a surrogate mother, they are soothed and their initial response diminishes. By contrast, the infant of four or five months is likely to show a high level of ongoing distress in the absence of his mother.

For a child aged six months to two-and-a-half years, the separation triggers the beginnings of grief and mourning. Shock is followed by protest in an attempt to have his mother back. As time passes and mummy doesn't return, the child becomes frustrated, realising at last that his protests are to no avail. His despair rises and yearning and pain ensue. He then goes into periods of withdrawal during which he engages in distracting activities and attempts to lose himself in play rather than tolerate the feelings of longing for extended periods. Eventually he gives up looking for his mother, abandons hope of her return and becomes sad.

The warning signs in this stage are a lack of interest in objects and activities that would ordinarily bring pleasure. This natural separation response will continue until a caring person steps in to fill the painful void. At first the infant may seem inconsolable, no matter how much comfort and consolation is offered: he simply wants his mum. It is through a persistent pattern of nurturing and comforting that his pain will eventually ease. The key is ongoing support despite the child's signals that it seems unwelcome at times.

This process of letting go and working towards the reality of loss applies to bereavement at any time of life but never so poignantly as at this early stage. Children do not have the advantage of maturity and knowledge from which we, as adults, may draw. And so we must assume the responsibility of being informed, recognising the signs of distress and intervening on behalf of our children. Often the intervention may involve a professional.

Week 34
A Three to Five-year Old's Grief

By the age of three a child's grief process is much the same as an adult's with one major difference - a little person's inability to process and verbalise his thoughts and feelings. This point is important to note lest we perceive a lack of communication as a sign that children are relatively unaffected by the death. They simply do not understand what is happening and eventually start to ask seemingly inappropriate questions. They are bewildered and often exhibit regressive behaviour, become demanding and clinging as they were earlier in their lives. Bed wetting and thumb sucking are examples of such regression. The child continues to question his mother's whereabouts and protests angrily when she does not return. In this confused state she may become attached to transitional objects, such as blankets and soft toys, and react angrily when they are taken away for laundering. We need not worry about this object dependence, however, for as time passes and adjustment begins, these items will lose their importance and appeal just as they do for children who are not suffering a loss.

Preoccupation with the deceased is normal, and children will benefit from frequent reviews of their relationship with the lost loved one. In the movie *Sleepless in Seattle* there is a scene where dad and son speak of the absent mom. Together they recall her bedtime song, along with other scenarios that bring them to tears.

By contrast, I met a woman, adopted at age three, whose birth mother was never seen or spoken of. One day she came across a model in a Sears catalogue, which triggered memories of her mum. The adoptive parents, interpreting the child's habit of looking through the book as obsessive and unhealthy, tore out the page and threw it away. Sadly the little girl spent hours leafing through the catalogue in search of that particular picture until one day the whole book disappeared. Her last hope of dealing with her loss had gone! At that point she withdrew further into her own little world of which any information about her birth mother was not a part.

The questions grieving children ask are normal and predictable. Next week we will look at answers that are commonly given and their interpretation.

Week 35
Answering a Child's Questions

"Where has mummy gone?" - a simple, direct question. Here are some typical answers and a child's reaction to them.

"Mummy has gone on a long trip." The child may feel abandoned and resentful that her mother left without telling her or, better still, taking her along. She may feel guilty and wonder if she was the cause of the abrupt leave taking. Obviously, too, this response conveys a false sense of hope that mummy will return some day.

"Daddy was so good that God wanted him." The boy, who also needed his dad, may feel angry. He may feel confused when he sees others sad and crying. As well, he may develop a fear of being good in case the god who the adults talk about decides to whisk him away too.

"Auntie was sick and died." This explanation sounds reasonable and harmless but without further explanation has its drawbacks. The child may then associate all sickness with death, fearing for himself and other loved ones.

"Grandma has gone to sleep forever." This answer may give rise to an association between sleep and death, causing obvious problems at bedtime and the development of sleep disturbances.

While these answers and their effects may seem far fetched, they have been well documented and verified. While we may be tempted to protect children by resorting to fairy tales and myths, explanations must be gentle and honest. The news should be relayed as soon as possible lest the child hear the facts, right or wrong, from another source. Speak in a normal tone of voice; whispered messages may give death a spooky, unreal connotation. Approach the child in a familiar and secure environment. It is important that we offer honest explanations that convey the irreversibility of the death. As permanence is a difficult concept for children to grasp, we might use an analogy of a broken toy that we wish we could fix but know we cannot.

Above all a child needs to know he's loved and will be cared for. Warn him that he will feel sad for a while and allow him to cry and to talk about his feelings as well as the person he is missing. Give reassurance that these uncomfortable feelings will not last forever.

Week 36
Emotional Benefits of the Funeral

Many bereaved people report having difficulty remembering the details of a the funeral. This limited recall is largely a result of the state of shock in which we first find ourselves. But no matter how much we can or cannot remember, a funeral or memorial service serves several important emotional purposes.

Visitation at the funeral home, and the service itself, are the beginnings of acceptance of the death. While in the denial stage we are unlikely to experience psychological acceptance, but there is no denying the setting: the casket, the grave and friends who have gathered to pay their respects and offer support. Later on even scant memories will help confirm the reality of the loss. In the case of a closed casket it is not unusual for family members to request a private viewing of their loved one simply to begin to grasp reality.

Funerals offer the survivors an opportunity to express their feelings and recall intimate memories of the deceased. Each time a story is told or an incident recounted, we move one small step forward towards resolving our loss.

A major component of the grief process is accepting the changed relationship with our loved one. The physical presence and interaction that once was exists no more, and a new relationship, based on memory and recollection, begins to form. Without the ritual of the funeral we may spend more time denying the truth.

We need to know that our loved one was well thought of in the community, to which tributes given at the funeral can attest. With kind words and assurance of how much the person will be missed, our loss has been validated and our grief legitimised.

The emotional benefits of a funeral apply to children considered mature enough to be given the option to attend. A decision to decline needs to be respected and, perhaps later on, a visit to the grave site might be useful in helping the child begin to come to grips with his loss.

Week 37
Reactions of Older Children

Children, by age five, begin to understand the gravity of death and its impact; but due to their immaturity and lack of coping skills, they work hard to deny the loss. When their feelings begin to surface they tend to cry in private. They may also fantasise that their loved one is still alive. However, they eventually become frustrated and realise their fantasies fall short of life before the loss.

A child of eight to twelve years has a similar reaction and works even harder to hide his feelings in an attempt to appear grown up. As he acknowledges the finality and irreversibility of death, his fearful feelings might manifest as anger. His behaviour, then, may be mislabelled as difficult. It is important to recognise the source of his acting out and encourage communication.

Grieving adolescents also might regress to a life stage where they felt a sense of safety and protection from death and its consequences - an escape route that could spawn inner conflict should they feel responsible for comforting family members. Their response to loss is much like an adult's, but typical issues, such as difficulty communicating other than with peers, heightened emotionality and ongoing issues of identity and independence, further complicate their grief. While teenagers work on the business of growing up they are likely to delay their grieving, but their pain may be recognised as exaggerated adult behaviours, withdrawal, depression and sexual acting out.

Four main factors influence a child's grief response: the family relationship patterns before the loss, especially those between the child and deceased; the causes and circumstances of the death; what he was told; and the extent to which the death changes family life.

Next week we will summarise the ways adults can help children deal with the trauma of loss.

Week 38
Helping Children Work Through Grief

Having briefly covered the grief responses of children of varying ages, we might keep in mind the following points as we help them to resolve their loss. These suggestions are particularly relevant when the death is that of a parent.

Take into account the child's age and stage of cognitive development, and communicate appropriately. Honesty is the best policy when discussing death and its consequences; simple, factual explanations are best in the long run.

Express your own grief openly and unashamedly. When children see adults cry they are more likely to let their own tears flow. The idea that adults need to put on a brave face for the sake of the children is a fallacy.

Observe the child's behaviour and note any apparent lack of concern. Children work hard to deny death, but their outward signs of calm probably do not reflect their feelings.

Nonverbal behaviour can reveal much about a child's state of mind and stage of grief. Pick up clues by observing behaviour in play. Art is an especially revealing medium through which children convey and work through feelings. Set a positive tone and talk about the absent parent. By sharing your feelings about the loss you set a good example, and he may follow suit.

Help the young child to remember his parent using pictures, possessions and stories. He can draw on these memories as he works towards accepting the loss of physical presence. This is where a memory box could help.

Give the child a sense of safety and security. In the aftermath of major change and loss, consistency is the key.

Be aware of any new tasks that children might take on. When they assume the role of man of the house or little mother, they may postpone their grief process indefinitely.

Children dealing with normal adolescence issues may need additional help to deal with their loss. Overall, though, children's needs are much like an adult's: validation of their feelings and pain; time; and an environment that allows for ample opportunity to grieve.

Week 39
The Death of a Child

When a child dies we find ourselves dealing with emotions that are unique to the abrupt separation of parent and child. The main factor in child death is its unnaturalness; children are the future generation and logically their lives should carry on after ours have ended. When this natural order is upset, parents and other family members must deal with the question of why this has happened. The search for answers is futile, and the lack of comprehension complicates and lengthens our grief process and raises the issue of survivor guilt.

Another issue with child death is the loss of the parental role that we assume when our children are born. Our task is to love and nurture our offspring, to keep them safe, happy and healthy - basically to watch over them until they reach maturity and independence. When we are deprived of this role our sense of loss is compounded and, because each of our children is unique and special, the death of one child even in a large family is devastating. As well, issues of parenting the remaining children need to be addressed.

The age at which a child dies is often of little relevance to a parent's grief; even in the case grown children who have moved away from home, the severing of the parent-child bond is an inconceivable circumstance. Other issues include the reactions of friends who are parents themselves, and the way in which a child's death impacts the parental relationship.

As with any bereavement situation, the closer we come to understanding our reactions and emotions, the better equipped we are to cope. All of the issues outlined above will be touched upon in the next few weeks.

Week 40
Age of the Child... What Matter?

Parents view the lost child's age as irrelevant and academic; they have lost their baby and an integral part of themselves, their dreams and expectations. The fact that a child has died out of turn overrides all other aspects of a parent's grief. However, there are some secondary, age-related issues that need to be acknowledged.

Adolescents tend to have a sense of immortality and often take risks that sometimes result in premature death. The sudden and dramatic circumstances of accidental death increase parental trauma and compound feelings of loss. Another complicating factor around adolescent death is the normal ambivalence that parents may feel during the tumultuous teen years; a teenager's rebellious behaviour may give rise to a parent's mixed emotions that manifest as regret.

The pain of parents of adult children is sometimes sadly minimised. Following the funeral of an only child, aged 43, it was rumoured that the parents' outpouring of grief was excessive and inappropriate, and that it upstaged the grief of the deceased's wife and children. I concluded that the remarks were made not out of malice but through a lack of knowledge of the complexities of grief. The bottom line: a parent is always a parent.

Societal fear and denial of death may cause us to shy away, albeit subconsciously, from mourners and particularly those who grieve for a child. When the parents' pain continues relentlessly, others may become anxious and realise that such an incomprehensible tragedy could befall their own family. Thankfully this gap in social and emotional backup is now being bridged through the formation of support groups.

Often the founding members of such groups and organisations are bereaved parents who found solace through sharing their pain and discussing aspects of child death, one of which is the subject of next week's column - parenting the remaining children.

Week 41
Parenting the Remaining Children

The siblings of a deceased brother or sister need parental love, attention and support. On the one hand, the presence of remaining children can be a great comfort; while grieving parents continue to fulfil their roles and perform familiar duties, they have a sense of purpose and motivation to carry on. On the other hand, the remaining children serve as constant reminders of the one who is missing, triggering painful memories.

Preoccupation with the deceased child makes for difficult parenting; for a mother or father consumed by sadness and a yearning for the physical presence of the lost child, commonplace tasks loom large. Energy ebbs, leaving the parent emotionally and physically drained.

Thinking purely good thoughts of the child is a normal reaction; however, as we work through our grief we begin to think more realistically and admit that the child, though lovable and loved, was not perfect. Meanwhile the remaining children, who are doing their best to fill the void, might feel resentful of the idealisation of their sibling, giving rise to the issue of a duality of response - simultaneous animosity and intense sadness.

We cannot conceive of one of our children dying, but once the unthinkable actually happens our fear is of history repeating itself. As natural and right as it is that we do everything in our power to protect each of our precious children, we need to be aware of the tendency to over protect them. This impulse surfaces most noticeably in parents who dwell on the things they did or did not do, for they have allowed their musings to cross the line to self-blame. This sense of heightened responsibility may spill over onto the siblings.

In a two-parent family, mum and dad have the advantage of a partnership through which they can work together and share concerns and tasks. However, the dynamics of grief can test any relationship to the limits.

Week 42
The Parents' Relationship

When tragedy hits, a community rallies together in a common cause to re-organise, rebuild and heal. And when death hits a family, its members, numbed and sad, become a close-knit supportive group. Ideally this spirit of togetherness will continue in the aftermath of the funeral when shock gives way to reality and each spouse becomes a source of strength for the other.

When a child dies, parents who look to each other for support in any other circumstance simultaneously begin to grieve this overwhelming loss. But the normal emotions of sadness, anger, depression and guilt may surface in ways that are counter productive to marital closeness and mutual support. For example, if the child's mother awakens feeling the need to talk, she might tearfully approach her partner in her need to share her pain. At the same time he may be trying desperately to control his emotions for any one of many reasons: he could be preparing for a challenging day at work; he may have had a hard time the previous day and needs an emotional reprieve; or he may simply be feeling numb. In any of these cases, his wife may misinterpret his apparent lack of emotion as a sign of callousness.

When one half of the marital dyad is feeling up and the other down, issues of a lack of synchronicity emerge, giving rise to a situation that, though common, has the potential to create an atmosphere of bewilderment and disappointment. The spouse who is having a down day may respond emotionally and instinctively, misdirecting anger (silent or aggressive) onto the partner. It is important, therefore, that bereaved parents gain some knowledge of the grief process; when they understand the dynamics of bereavement, they might communicate more effectively and, in so doing, be more supportive of one another.

Week 43
Gender Differences in Grief Work

Bereaved parents will be disappointed if they expect their grief responses and stages to match, and some differences are a result of lost roles. A mother who spent her days caring for a child will be painfully aware of the absence of the youngster's physical presence; the touching, cuddling, feeding, talking and listening are gone. A father misses many aspects of his child but at varying times, such as after work or on the weekend when it was his turn to spend quality time with his child, perhaps at the park or sports arena. Each parent will experience feelings off loss in different ways and at different times.

Although times are changing, sex-role socialisation affects the way in which men and women handle grief. Traditionally - and I offer the following comments as mere generalisations - women have been socialised to express the sort of emotions naturally expressed in grief work. Bereaved mums are likely to have ample opportunity to talk and to cry in the company of other women. Men are less likely to share their feelings, and even if the time and place are right, social expectation could serve to control emotions and tears. These differences may put the couple completely out of sync.

While parents invest time and energy in grieving, other relationship issues may be put on the back burner. When not addressed, the day-to-day trivia tends to accumulate and add to the weight and stress of grief. The danger, then, is that one or both partners will have a bursting of their emotional wall resulting in possible misunderstandings and heightened feelings of helplessness, loss and isolation.

To say that the death of a child is a major life crisis would be to make an understatement to beat all! But it bears repeating that such a devastating loss cannot help but effect change in the parents and their relationship. By communicating and giving each other permission to grieve as individuals, bereaved parents can make it to the top of their mountains and on down the other side, united and strong in their precious shared memories of the child they loved and lost.

Week 44
On New Paths...

The grief process, thoroughly and objectively studied and documented by researchers and clinicians, is comprised of a series of stages: shock and denial, anger, depression, acceptance and renewed hope. Having many times bounced back and forth between the phases, I can attest to their validity and now take the liberty of summarising the journey from a personal point of view, using my *new paths* framework.

Numbness - when our minds shut down lest they explode from the pressure of the truth: he is gone and will never return.

Emotions - sadness, despair, anger, yearning, guilt - ever changing, confusing, overwhelming.

Work - the hardest imaginable, even beyond imagination - and yet it is work that must be done.

Patience, perseverance, and prayer to bear the pain; pacing ourselves while reaching outwards and upwards for support and guidance.

Acceptance of reality; an awareness of the complexities of grief; anticipating the highs and lows and, at long last, moving on.

Time alone does not heal, but as we face grief head on we will heal the hurt.

Hope in the future; that seed of faith planted deep within will bring us through the dark days and out into the light.

Seeing - not just looking but really seeing the wondrous beauty of our world: bursting buds, soft green shoots piercing through a blanket of dead leaves; robins gathering straw for their nests; the sun, moon and stars and knowing there is so much more than meets the eye and that passes our human understanding.

The death of a loved one leads us along new paths, literally and spiritually. My new direction was to the top of a metaphorical mountain, and I doggedly clung onto that image as I travelled through frightening and unfamiliar territory. Eventually I found a peaceful new path and, as was the case with Pandora's otherwise empty box, discovered that human hope is eternal.

Week 45
And on Down the Other Side

"Life is like walking down a wooded trail, trying to guess where you're going from the markers left behind!" - a profound statement shared with me by a friend.

I would like to believe that for everything that happens in life there is a reason, even though it eludes us at the time. Only now, as I look back over the past two years, do I begin to recognise the rightness of our move eight months after Mike's sudden death. Our country home in its quiet setting turned out to be the perfect place to begin our healing.

One day while wandering through the bush and thinking about the rollercoaster ride on which I was a reluctant passenger, I made some notes; I needed to make some sense of my mood swings, the futility and yet hope, and the changes that had occurred in so short a time. It dawned on me then that I might help myself and others by sharing my experiences and newfound knowledge. Thus my column was born, written for the most part on a grassy bank by the creek. Was it coincidence that my writings appeared in the same newspaper through which we found our farmhouse? I think not! Nor is it a coincidence that I pen the last two columns as the girls and I prepare to leave our country home.

I will never understand why my son had to die, but I do know that the trails I forged through the Jarvis bush have led me a fair distance up my mountain path. Still I have work to do to reach that peak and place of peace, and I'm drawn to another place to continue the hard work. Again my daughters and I move on in faith, not knowing exactly where or why but trusting that our destination and the tasks awaiting us will become clear in time.

In my final column of the series I leave you with a short piece that was read at my son's memorial service. May its message, as I hope has been my writing, be a source of comfort and inspiration for all who suffer the pain of loss through death.

Week 46
A Fond Farewell

Dudley Cavert in *Beyond Sorrow* wrote the following piece, edited by Herb and Mary Montgomery. Its message, for me, is all the more profound given the amount of time I spent sitting beside the creek.

"In the bottom of an old pond lived some grubs who could not understand why none of their group ever came back after crawling up the stems of the lilies to the top of the water.

They promised each other that the next one who was called to make the upward climb would return and tell what happened to him. Soon one of them felt an urgent impulse to seek the surface: he rested himself on top of a lily pad and went through a glorious transformation which made him a dragonfly with beautiful wings.

In vain he tried to keep his promise. Flying back and forth over the pond, he peered down at his friends below. Then he realised that even if they could see him, they would not recognise such a radiant creature as one of their number.

The fact that we cannot see our friends or communicate with them after the transformation which we call death is no proof that they cease to exist."

This column series is dedicated to my son, Michael Paul Phillips.

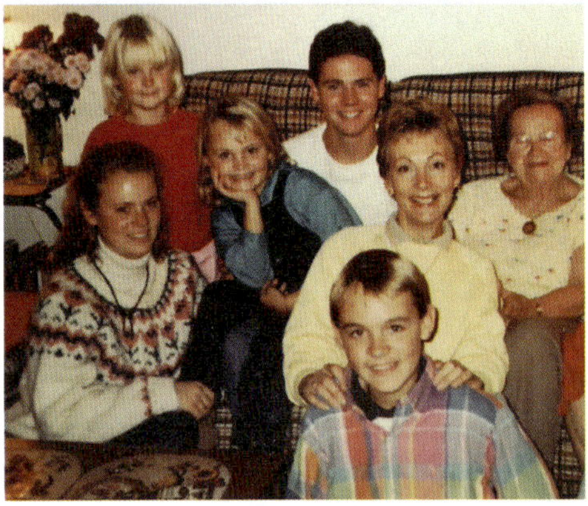

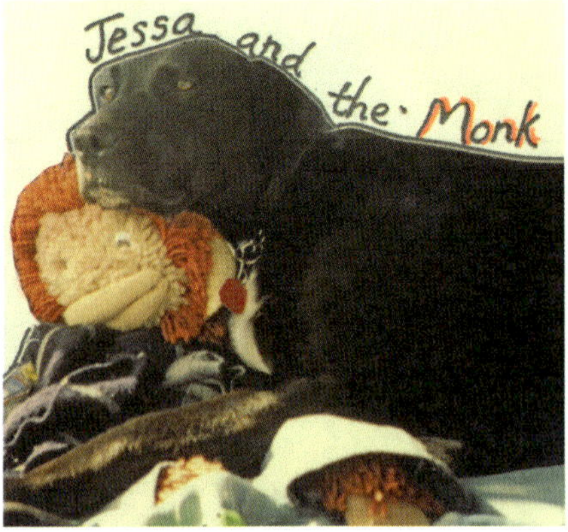
Jessa and the Monk

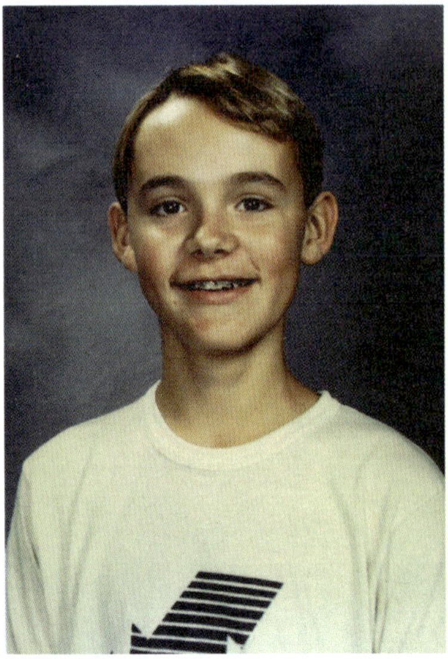

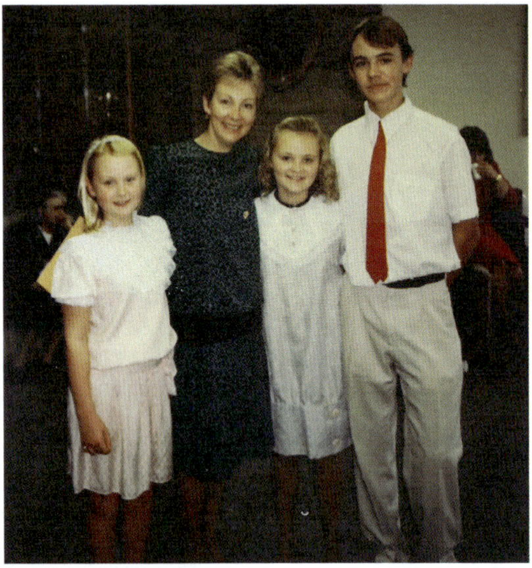

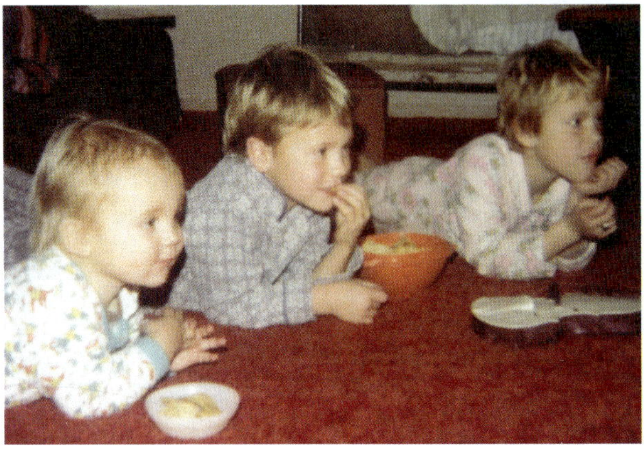

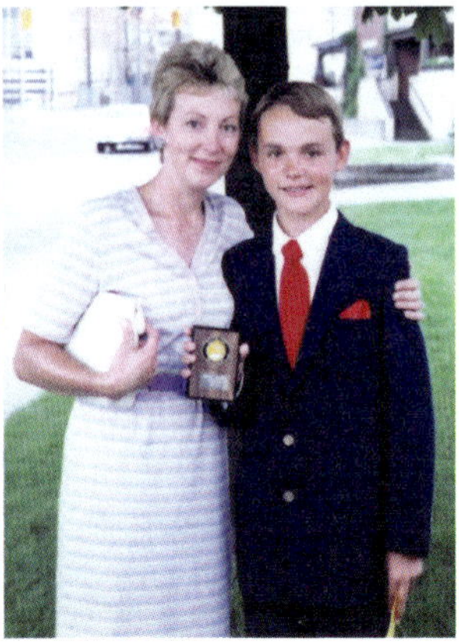

Acknowledgements

In creating this book I've had the crucial benefit of others who have experienced and/or studied grief, as well as many authors who, in a general sense, have added to my knowledge and, indeed, to the understanding of my own grief journey.

Along the way I found several agencies specifically concerned with helping people through grief and bereavement.

My first port of call, soon after Mike's death, was *Bereaved Families of Ontario*. Also, more recently, following Angi's passing, I sought help through two UK agencies - *Cruse* and *The Compassionate Friends*.

All of the volunteers and workers within these three organisations aided me in ways beyond all expectation. My hope is that through this book I am able to give back and help others in grief.

I know how important a support system is to those who have suffered loss; family members and good friends have stood by me in bad times and good. My love and gratitude goes out to each of them.

A special thank you to 'Nige' Kendall who encouraged me to finally get around to compiling and completing this book. His skills in publication design brought order and colour to an otherwise confusing and sombre subject.

If you have any comments or questions please contact me on:
ivyhousefarm@gmail.com

Made in the USA
Columbia, SC
20 December 2017